A Visual Approach to Functions

Frances Van Dyke

Key Curriculum Press
Innovators in Mathematics Education

Project Editor Ladie Malek
Editorial Consultants Ema M. Arcellana, Mary Jo Cittadino
Editorial Assistants Christopher David, Heather Dever, Jason Taylor
Production Editors Kristin Ferraioli, Jacqueline Gamble
Copyeditor Margaret Moore
Editorial Production Manager Deborah Cogan
Production Director Diana Jean Parks
Production Coordinators Laurel Roth Patton, Jenny K. Somerville
Text Designer Burl Sloan
Compositor Christi Payne
Art Editor Jason Luz
Illustrator Juan Alvarez
Technical Artist Tom Webster
Art and Design Coordinator Caroline Ayres
Cover Designer Jenny K. Somerville
Cover Photos ©Roy Ooms, Masterfile; ©Erik Aeden, Image State

Executive Editor Casey FitzSimons
Publisher Steven Rasmussen

Key Curriculum Press
1150 65th Street
Emeryville, CA 94608
editorial@keypress.com
http://www.keypress.com

Printed in the United States of America   10 9 8 7 6 5 4 3 2   09 08 07 06 05 04
ISBN 1-55953-537-7

Contents

Introduction

This work is intended for students who are beginning algebra as well as for those who have studied it for a year or more. After publishing *A Visual Approach to Algebra*, teachers I talked to felt they needed material that would incorporate a visual approach with more traditional curriculum. In this book I concentrate on developing a series of visual exercises to introduce some of the standard functions and applications that students encounter in algebra.

Students will benefit a great deal from exploring the relationship between a graph and a verbal statement describing a function before looking at a table or an algebraic representation. When trying to understand the subtle notion of a function it seems most natural to start by looking at a qualitative graph that describes the relationship between two quantities. Working directly with the graphs and the statement will draw students into the application, start them thinking abstractly, and lead them toward an understanding of algebraic concepts before having to deal with algebraic notation.

A visual approach has long-term as well as immediate benefits. In our technology-rich society, graphic representations of problems and events are ever more common, and it is increasingly important that students be able to interpret, compare, and create graphs. To understand underlying concepts in calculus, students need basic visual thinking skills. Graphing calculators and a new emphasis on graphs allow us to introduce certain important ideas from calculus at an earlier point in the curriculum, and this will consequently make the calculus course more accessible. In this book students are often asked questions about rates of change, intervals of increase and decrease, and global behavior.

In the past several years many articles have been written urging us to make functions a central theme of high school algebra. It has been convincingly argued that students will learn mathematics best if it is presented in the context of a meaningful application. We have been invited to explore concepts with our students verbally, numerically, visually, and algebraically. In the case of a function, this corresponds to looking at a verbal description along with a table of values, a graph, and an algebraic expression that describes the relationship.

Students will indeed gain a deep understanding of functions if they can master these representations and understand the underlying equivalence. Equivalence, however, is often elusive. When two things look different, the natural tendency is to see them as unrelated, and the notion of fundamental equivalence is easily lost. This is true when students are manipulating algebraic equations as well as when moving from one representation to another. Just as it is essential to understand properties of equality when students are working with algebraic equations, it is imperative to explore equivalence in all the directions indicated in the figure below.

In the traditional curriculum, certain of these directions are emphasized far more than others. Verbal description to algebraic representation, algebraic representation to table, and table to graph have been standard exercises for the past century. In this book all the

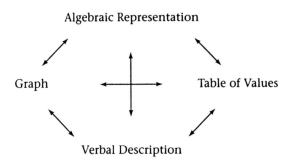

directions are covered, taking into account the difficulty students have in recognizing equivalence. Questions such as "What is the effect on the y-intercept given a change in the situation described?" force students to mentally adjust the graph given altered circumstances. Templates that show graph, equation, table, and statement simultaneously are also used to help tie different representations together.

In spite of the fact that it makes good sense to teach mathematics in context, and that we hope to generate more enthusiasm for the subject using this approach, we still encounter many students with a dislike for word problems. In the past we expected our students to go immediately from the verbal description to the algebraic representation. More recently, students have been building up a table of values, looking at patterns, and then producing the correct algebraic expression. It is the purpose of this book to lead students to an understanding of functions using a different approach. We concentrate on the relationship between the graph and the verbal description before considering the table or equation. In the case of linear functions, the slope and intercepts can be interpreted and understood without the equation. This will help students who have a difficult time with the algebraic representation. Thinking about the graph and exploring in depth the relationship between the graph and the verbal description is a good intermediate step to take before attempting the more abstract job of working with equations.

The book consists of six chapters: two concentrating on linear functions, two on exponential, and two on quadratic. Every chapter has one or two central themes, allowing students to become thoroughly comfortable with applications associated with particular themes. It is my belief that a dislike of word problems stems from difficulty with them, and that complete familiarity with certain functions can go a long way toward rectifying students' reluctance to attack word problems. Each chapter consists of exercise sheets along with teacher notes. The notes give answers, ideas for incorporating graphing calculators, and indications of the pedagogical intent and potential problems students may experience.

All chapters start with exercises on qualitative graphs; students are given a series of sentences and in each case are asked to pick the graph that best matches the sentence. They need to understand how the two principal quantities are related and how this relationship is pictured abstractly using coordinate axes. They must have an overall view of the relationship. They must be able to orient the graph in the correct fashion, keeping in mind that the independent quantity increases as you move to the right along the x-axis, while the dependent quantity increases as you move up along the y-axis. This is a valid exercise for both pre-algebra and algebra students and is a natural way for students to start thinking about the theme under study. They go on to describe a relationship given a graph, compare two relationships based on their graphs, and draw an appropriate graph given a particular relationship. The situations increase in complexity, but the graphs remain qualitative.

Once the relationship has been presented using qualitative graphs, it is natural to introduce coordinates and start looking at quantitative graphs. At this stage, particular situations corresponding to the application are specified, and the students must interpret given coordinates in terms of the situation. Again, the exercises move from the graph to the verbal situation, as well as from sentence to graph. Points on the graph indicate details of a situation that the students are asked first to record and then to create. This work makes the ensuing exercises with tables and equations more meaningful and easier to comprehend. Pre-algebra teachers may use this material as well.

From quantitative graphs we go on to tables. Students learn to move in the six directions indicated above, among tables, graphs, and statements. Seeing a pattern allows them to interpolate and make new statements about given situations as well as about situations they come up with themselves.

The final exercises in each unit incorporate algebraic notation and contain challenging exercises. Teachers may decide not to use all of these depending on the class. Once the algebraic notation has been introduced, the earlier exercises with quantitative graphs and tables may be revisited and students can be asked to give the appropriate algebraic representations.

For the last decade I have written material for teachers that promotes using a visual approach in the classroom. Many of us were trained in mathematics with very little emphasis on diagrams or graphs. Despite the widespread use of graphing calculators today, research shows that high school students still tend to rely on algebraic representations and are very reluctant to use a graph when given a choice. Introducing functions by moving from qualitative graphs to quantitative graphs, then to tables, then to equations has many advantages. Starting with qualitative graphs helps students think on an abstract level and allows the teacher to introduce concepts from algebra without the burden of algebraic notation. The transfer from qualitative to quantitative graphs is easy and deepens the understanding of the relationship between the quantities depicted. Students start to come up with other values for the function on their own and have no trouble shifting to a table of values. The equation is appropriately presented last, as it is the most abstract representation for the relationship. It is my hope that all who use this work will gain from it and enjoy it.

This book is dedicated to my husband, Ted, to my three children, Chris, Hugo, and Mary, and to the memory of two other Hugos and two Nancys.

Frances Van Dyke
American University
Washington, D.C.

Graphing Calculator Notes

You will find graphing calculator activities at the end of each chapter. The activities are meant to complement and reinforce what students learn in each lesson. They can be photocopied, cut apart, and incorporated into each lesson, or done a page at a time every few days. Calculator Activity descriptions and answers can be found in the Extension sections of the Teacher's Notes.

These notes apply to many of the Calculator Activities throughout the book. You may want to discuss them with students as they do the Calculator Activities.

Show students how to use the Window settings to view a sufficient portion of the graph. Many of the applications make sense only in the first quadrant. Have students set the minimum values at 0.

Discuss how to view table settings and how to change x and y intervals in the table.

Show students how to use the Enter key to change the highlighting on the equal sign in order to view only one or two graphs at a time.

Show students how to trace along a graph using the left and right arrows, and jump between graphs using the up and down arrows.

Depending on the window they are using, students may not be able to trace exactly to a specific number, due to the number of pixels on the screen. It is possible to trace to a specific x-value by typing in the number and pressing Enter. Otherwise, for clean trace values, find out the pixel width of the screen and take a convenient fraction of that for your x-interval length.

An easy way to create a graph of a piecewise function on a graphing calculator is to use lists. In STAT mode, enter the x- and y-coordinates in separate lists (L1 and L2). From the STAT PLOT menu, select a connected scatter plot. Graph the function.

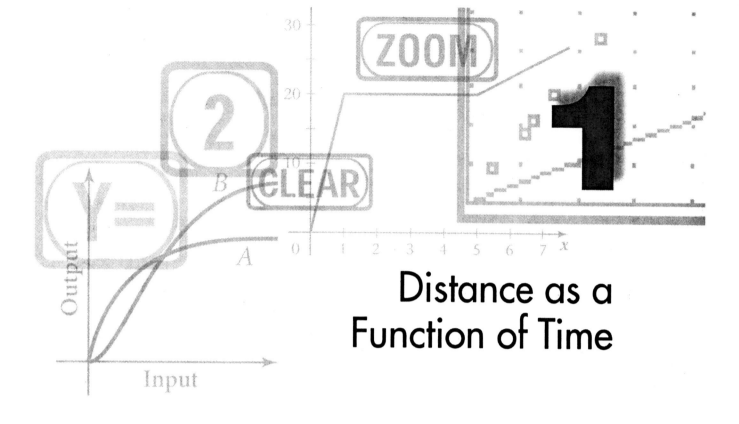

Distance as a Function of Time

This chapter introduces functions through the simple and tangible application of distance as a function of time. Students begin by studying graph sketches, or qualitative graphs, in Lessons 1–4, and by focusing on the shapes of the graphs. They slowly progress to quantitative graphs with some coordinates marked, in Lessons 5–7. Then, in Lessons 8–13, they begin to work with tables and equations. Lessons 14 and 15 focus on piecewise functions, sometimes considered an advanced topic, yet very accessible when related to real-life situations. Lesson 16 can be used as a review or challenge.

If a motion detector is available, it complements this chapter nicely. Optional activities using graphing calculators are included at the end of the chapter. Some of these also require a motion detector.

Lesson 1

Walking at a Steady Pace

Each sentence tells how far a person is from an object. Choose the graph that shows the person's distance from the object as time goes by.

1. Hugo walked away from the car.

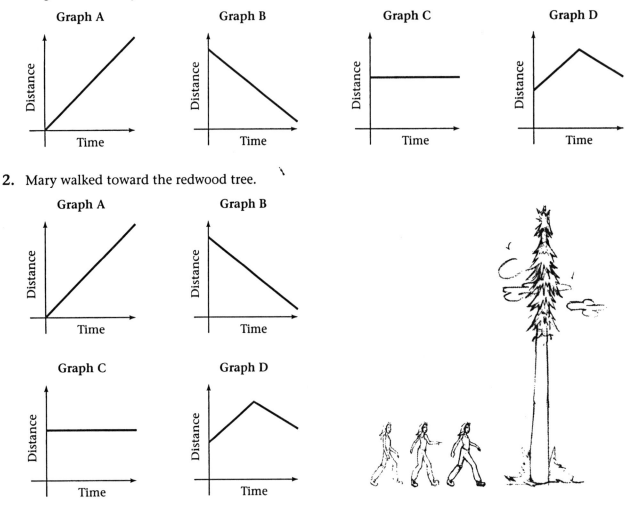

2. Mary walked toward the redwood tree.

3. Nancy first ran toward the slide and then away from it.

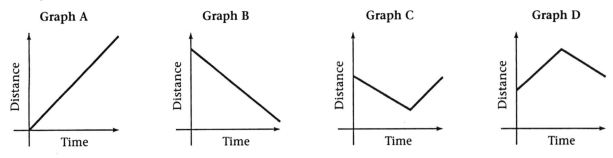

A Visual Approach to Functions / © 2002 Key Curriculum Press

TEACHER NOTES

The objective of Lessons 1 and 2 is for students to understand very simple graphical representations of distance from an object, over time. For now, we talk about "distance over time," but this relationship can also be called "distance versus time" or "distance as a function of time."

Remind students that to show time going by, you move to the right on the graph, and to show distance getting greater, you move up on the graph. Students must be able to orient this relationship in the correct fashion so that by the end of Lesson 1, they make the connection between what the graph shows and what is happening in real terms. Students should understand that when distance increases on the graph, it means the person is moving away from the object and when distance decreases on the graph, it means the person is moving closer to the object.

One way to use this lesson is to first let students do Lesson 1 followed by Calculator Activity 1, and then allow them to revise their answers to Lesson 1 before it is corrected. If students are unclear on a question, letting them model it with the motion detector might help their understanding.

Answers

1. Graph A   2. Graph B   3. Graph C

Extension: See Calculator Activity 1 _____

Hands-on experience with a motion detector can help students to comprehend graphs of distance over time. You may want to model this activity with the whole class before letting students work in groups or with partners.

$\mathcal{Lesson\ 2}$

Moving Around the Museum

Each sentence tells how far a person is from an object. Decide which graph matches the sentence. In Questions 1, 2, and 4 the "object" is a museum. In Question 3 it is a painting.

1. We walked at a steady pace toward the museum.

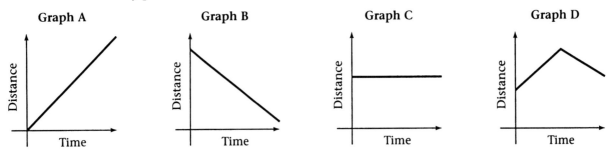

2. My sister ran away from the museum but came back when my parents called her.

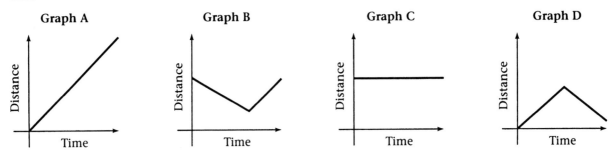

3. My father stood for a very long time in front of a painting.

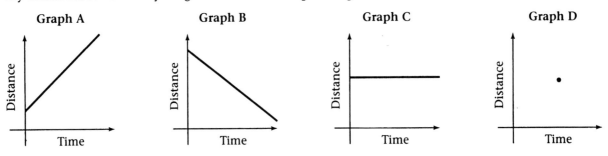

4. Afterward, we raced down the hill away from the museum. (Be careful here.)

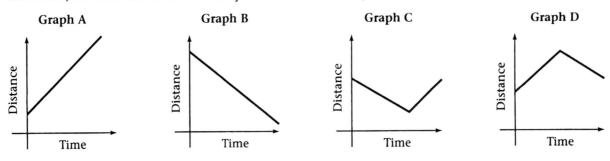

A Visual Approach to Functions / © 2002 Key Curriculum Press

TEACHER NOTES

This lesson gives students more practice looking at individual graphs and describing what is happening in each.

Often students think of the graph as simply a picture of the scene. Here this misconception may arise in Questions 3 and 4. In Question 3 many students will answer Graph D, thinking of the father as a stationary speck in front of the painting. In Question 4 the image of running down the hill will make Graph B a popular choice. It may help students to acknowledge that distance from the bottom of the hill decreases, but that distance from the museum increases.

If students are having trouble picturing how distance is changing (or staying constant), encourage them to sketch "snapshots" of the action with a running clock or stopwatch in the corner.

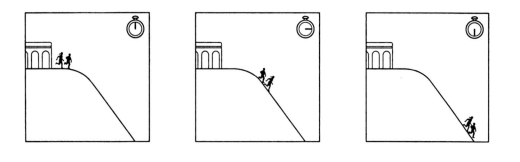

Answers

1. Graph B   2. Graph D   3. Graph C   4. Graph A

 ## Extension: See Calculator Activity 2 _____

In this activity, students try to reproduce the graphs from the lesson by using a motion detector and their own motion. Students gain a strong understanding of what the graphs represent and Question 2 clarifies the meaning of a horizontal line (which can be created by standing still) and of a vertical line (which is impossible to create).

Lesson 3
Comparing and Describing Motion

1. Everyone is walking directly toward or away from the school, or standing still. Each of the four graphs below shows motions for two separate people.

   a. Give each person a name that starts with the letter on the graph. For example, G and H could stand for Gina and Henry. Interpret each graph and write a few sentences, giving details about each person's motion. Make as many observations and comparisons as you can.

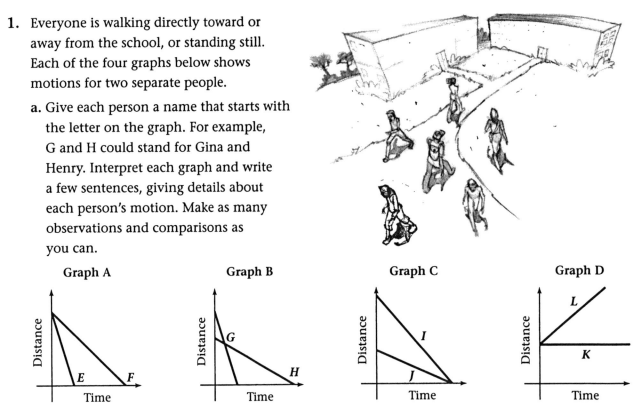

Graph A Distance / Time — E, F

Graph B Distance / Time — G, H

Graph C Distance / Time — I, J

Graph D Distance / Time — L, K

   b. Is it possible that the two people in Graph A are closer together when they have finished walking than they were at the start?

   c. Who is walking faster in each graph? Explain how you can tell.

2. Janet, Gail, and Susan all walked away from the railroad station. Janet walked at a steady pace. Gail realized she was late and sped up as she walked. Susan slowed down to look around. Decide which graph shows each girl's walk.

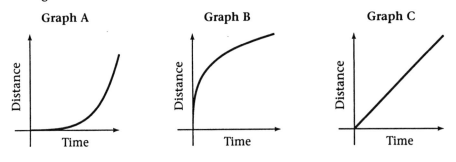

Graph A Distance / Time

Graph B Distance / Time

Graph C Distance / Time

A Visual Approach to Functions / © 2002 Key Curriculum Press

TEACHER NOTES

This lesson uses what students have learned in the two previous lessons. Students compare different graphs and interpret their meanings. In comparing two graphs, students will think about the starting distance (the *y*-intercept), the time it takes to arrive (the *x*-intercept), and the walking rate (the slope).

In Question 1, the reason for specifying that each person walks "directly toward or away from" the school is that, without knowing this, students cannot determine the rate. For example, a graph that shows a person staying at a constant distance from the school could mean a person is standing still *or* running in circles around the school.

In Graph A, some students may incorrectly think that one person walks a shorter distance than the other. Also, the distance between the two *x*-intercepts should not be interpreted as distance between the two walkers. They could end up at the exact same spot.

The curved graphs in Question 2 introduce students to increasing and decreasing rates of change, or "speeding up" and "slowing down." This is an important idea in calculus and often gives students trouble. You might use slope triangles to help your students understand how the distance covered changes over time in Graph A and Graph B and stays the same in Graph C.

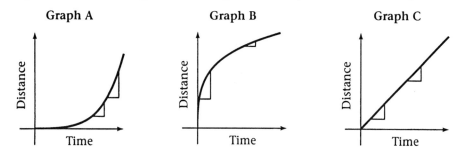

Answers

1. **a.** Graph A: E and F both start at the same distance from the school, but not necessarily at the same places, and walk toward the school. E walks faster than F and reaches the school sooner.

    Graph B: G and H both walk toward the school—G starts farther away and walks faster, reaching the school first; H starts closer but walks more slowly, reaching the school after G. At the point where their lines cross, G and H are the same distance from the school at the same time.

    Graph C: I and J are both walking toward the school. I starts farther away and walks faster; J starts closer and walks slower—they both reach the school at the same time.

    Graph D: K and L are both a certain distance away from the school. L walks farther away from the school; K stands still.

b. Yes. They both end up at school. Also, they started out at the same distance from school, but they could have come from opposite directions.

  c. In the first graph, E is walking at a faster rate, in the second graph it is G, in the third graph it is I, in the fourth graph it is L. The person with the steeper graph is always the one who is walking faster.

2. Graph B is for Susan, Graph A is for Gail, and Graph C is for Janet.

Extension: See Calculator Activity 3

Students will enter equations to obtain the graphs in these exercises, but they only need to come up with a verbal description to match the shape.

   The last question produces parabolas, which model the "speeding up" and "slowing down" that students saw in Question 2 from Lesson 3.

Lesson 4

Graphs with Different Sections

1. These graphs show the distances of four different airplanes from the airport from 8 A.M. to 9 A.M.

   Describe where each airplane was during that hour. Give as many details as you can. Put a scale along the *x*-axis of each graph and estimate times for each event.

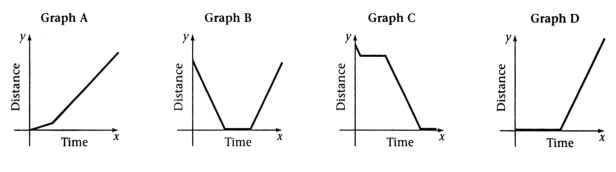

Graph A:

Graph B:

Graph C:

Graph D:

2. Draw a graph of distance and time for each of the following sentences. Label your graphs with "distance," "time," and the person's name.

   A. Carla walked a short way toward the sign, stood and looked at it for a while, and then walked away quickly.

   B. While she was waiting for her brother at the dentist's office, Jasmine ran away from the office, raced back to it, walked away slowly, and then ran back again.

   C. Ron walked away from the library, stopped to talk to a friend, and then hurried away to swim practice.

   D. Alex walked to the mailbox, stood for a while, walked away very slowly, and then stopped to talk to a neighbor.

TEACHER NOTES

This lesson starts to prepare students for the appearance of coordinates on a graph. Encourage students to write full sentences and come up with scenarios to explain what is happening in the graphs. Encourage them to be as specific as they can. A discussion of segments and piecewise graphs may help them break down the different parts of the motion.

This is also the first lesson where students are asked to draw graphs. The shift from recognizing an appropriate graph to producing a graph may be difficult for students. You may choose to do problems similar to these with the whole class before letting students do the lesson on their own.

Most students will probably draw simple straight-line graphs. Others may use curves to show speeding up or slowing down. Either method is fine, and you may discuss these options with the class if you wish.

You can also begin to teach the concept of a function and talk about horizontal and vertical lines on a graph. If students did Calculator Activity 2, you can discuss creating horizontal lines and the impossibility of making a vertical line. (The passage of time makes a vertical graph impossible.) You can also point out that for each moment in time, a person can only be at one particular distance from an object. This is what distinguishes a function from other relationships. Each element in the domain corresponds to one, and only one, element in the range. Or, in other words, no two points on the graph of a function can lie on the same vertical line.

Ask your students, "Can you be at the same distance from something at two different times?" (Yes.) "Can you be at two different distances from something at the same time?" (No—it's impossible to be in two different places at once!)

Answers

1. Sample answers:

   Graph A: The plane leaves the airport at 8 a.m. At around 8:15, the plane accelerates to a higher speed.

   Graph B: The plane arrives at around 8:20. After about 20 minutes, it takes off again.

   Graph C: The plane is approaching the airport. From around 8:10 to 8:30, it is either grounded at a nearby town or in a holding pattern over the airport. The plane finally arrives at around 8:50.

   Graph D: This plane takes off around 8:30.

2. A.   Carla   B.   Jasmine   C.   Ron   D.   Alex

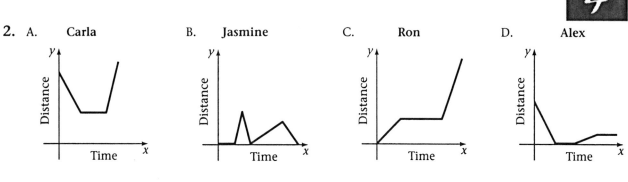

Extension: See Calculator Activity 4 _____

Answers to Calculator Activity

1. Student answers will vary. Some things that are alike: the person starts out and ends up at the object; when people are moving, the motion is steady (no speeding up or slowing down); there is a segment where the person stays at the same distance for a while; the maximum distance from the object is the same; the duration and rate in the first segment are the same. Some things that are different: the person stays at the same distance for a longer time in the second graph; the return to the object in the second graph is in a shorter time (because the same distance is covered, the rate must be faster).

2. Answers will vary. Sample answer: For the first graph, walk away from the detector, stand still for a bit, then walk back more quickly than you walked away. For the second graph, walk away as fast as you walked away for the first graph, to about the same place, then stand still for longer than the first time and walk back even more quickly than you did for the first graph.

Lesson 5
Moving Toward a Car, Part 1

This graph shows a woman's distance from a car over time.

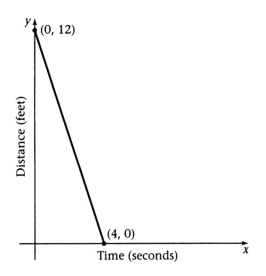

1. Which of these sentences is a good match for the graph above?

    A. A woman was 4 feet from a car and walked toward it, reaching the car after 12 seconds.

    B. A woman was 12 feet from a car and walked toward it at the rate of 4 feet per second.

    C. A woman was 12 feet from a car and walked toward it, reaching it after 4 seconds.

    D. A woman was 4 feet from a car and walked away from it, stopping after 3 seconds when she was 12 feet away.

2. How many feet did the woman walk in all? How long did it take her to walk this distance?

3. How far was the woman from the car after 1 second? After 2 seconds? After 3 seconds? How do you know?

4. How many feet did she walk in each second?

5. Write down the three sentences you did not choose in Question 1. Next to each one, draw a graph for it.

A Visual Approach to Functions / © 2002 Key Curriculum Press

TEACHER NOTES

This lesson introduces coordinates on the graph. Students interpret where the motion begins, how long it lasts, and the speed, all based on the *x*- and *y*-intercepts.

Answers

1. Sentence C

2. She walked 12 feet. It took 4 seconds.

3. She was 9 feet away after 1 second, 6 feet away after 2 seconds, and 3 feet away after 3 seconds. The straight line means a steady rate of walking.

4. She walked 3 feet per second.

5.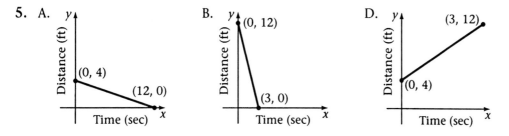

Extension: See Calculator Activity 5

This is an introductory exploration of coordinates and intercepts using a graphing calculator. For more practice (or just for effect), repeat the activity with the equation for a spider closing in on a trapped fly:

$$y = 30 - 2x$$

Answers to Calculator Activity

1. 20 centimeters away; (0, 20)

2. Answers will vary. Possible answers: (1, 19.5), (2, 19), (10, 15), (20, 10), (30, 5). Sample sentence: After 10 seconds, the beetle was 15 centimeters away from the lettuce.

3. It takes 40 seconds. That is where distance is 0. (40, 0).

Lesson 6

Identifying the Right Graph

For each sentence, choose the graph that matches the situation.

1. Carlos was standing 5 feet from the edge of the lake. He walked away from the lake for 3 seconds. Then he was 11 feet away from the lake.

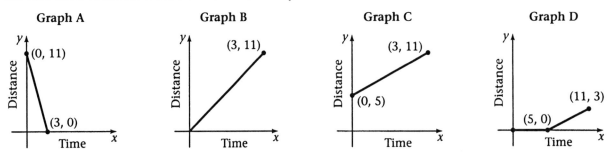

2. For each of the three graphs you didn't choose in Question 1, write a sentence or story to go with that graph.

3. Dana was standing 25 feet from the lake. She then walked toward it at a rate of 4 feet per second.

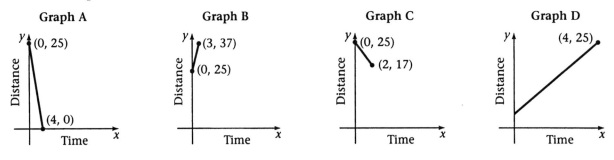

4. For each of the three graphs you didn't choose in Question 3, write a sentence or story to go with that graph.

   A Visual Approach to Functions / © 2002 Key Curriculum Press

TEACHER NOTES

Students start to practice looking at coordinates on a graph for clues about distance, time, and rate of travel. They try to match situations to graphs, basing their decisions on the appropriate numbers. Make sure students are thinking about the motion as a whole, and not just zeroing in on specific points.

You may choose to talk about the terms for the ideas students have learned so far: "function," "coordinates," "x-intercept," "y-intercept," "rate," and "slope." You might also ask students to share their methods for determining rate.

Answers

1. Graph C

2. Graph A: "Carlos started out 11 feet from the lake and reached it after 3 seconds."

   Graph B: "Carlos started out at the lake. After 3 seconds he was 11 feet from the lake."

   Graph D: "Carlos started out at the lake and stood there for 5 seconds. He then moved away and after 6 more seconds he was 3 feet away."

3. Graph C

4. Graph A: "Dana started out 25 feet from the lake. She walked toward it, and after 4 seconds she was at the lake."

   Graph B: "Dana started out 25 feet from the lake. She walked away, and after 3 seconds she was 37 feet away."

   Graph D: "Dana started out at a certain distance from the lake. She walked away from it, and after 4 seconds she was 25 feet from the lake."

Extension: See Calculator Activity 6

Students continue to practice by using TRACE to look at coordinates and drawing conclusions about distance, time, and speed. Question 5 guides students to explore noninteger values.

Answers to Calculator Activity

Answers should include several sentences giving the distance at different times, three of them for noninteger time values. The speed is 60 miles per hour.

Traveling Around

1. Each of the following graphs shows distance from an object as a function of time. Write a story that could go with each graph. Choose a person or an object for your story. Also choose units for distance (feet, centimeters, miles, etc.) and for time (seconds, minutes, hours, etc.) and describe the motion and the speed.

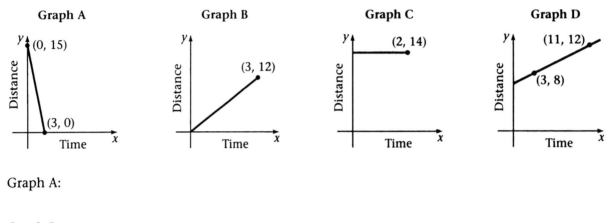

Graph A:

Graph B:

Graph C:

Graph D:

2. For each of the following sentences, make a graph that shows the distance over time. Remember to label your axes and put marks along them. Each piece of information in the sentence should correspond with a pair of coordinates on your graph. (For example, in sentence A, the train starts out at 30 meters away, so label (0, 30) on your graph.)

A. The train was 30 meters away from the station. It reached the station after 6 seconds.

B. Kathy drove away from the town. After 5 minutes she was 3 miles away, and she continued driving at that speed.

C. Jane stood 20 feet away from the shop for 3 seconds. She decided she didn't need anything and walked away. After 5 seconds she was 30 feet away.

D. The truck was 5 feet from the fire station. It started moving away, and after 3 seconds it was 15 feet away.

TEACHER NOTES

In this lesson, we begin to refer to "distance over time" as "distance as a function of time."

Graph D in Question 1 is the most difficult one and forces students to work backward to find the starting point. Finding rate from this graph is also more difficult. Encourage students to state everything they know from looking at the graph and to try to make these deductions. Thinking through these difficult ideas will help them better grasp formulas later on.

Point out that the scale along the x-axis may be vastly different than that along the y-axis. Once you have chosen a unit along a particular axis, you need to be consistent along that line. For example, in Graph C of Question 2, 20 should be two thirds of the way from 0 to 30 along the y-axis. This graph frequently gives students trouble and they may mislabel the y-intercept (3, 20).

Answers

1. The choice of person and object will vary, but answers should include

   Graph A: They started 15 units from the object and moved toward it at a rate of 5 distance units per time unit, reaching the object after 3 time units.

   Graph B: They started at the object and moved way from it at a rate of 4 units per time unit. After 3 time units, they were 12 units away.

   Graph C: They remained at a distance of 14 units from the object for 2 time units.

   Graph D: They started moving away. After 3 time units they were 8 units away from the object, and after 11 time units, 12 units away. This means they were walking at a rate of 0.5 distance unit per time unit. Therefore, they started out at 6.5 units away.

2.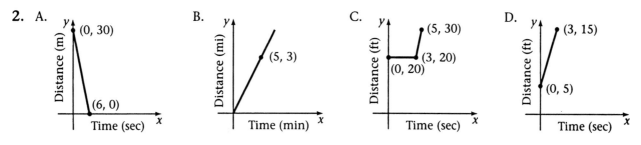

Extension: See Calculator Activity 7 _____

We continue working with the equation for a car moving at 60 mph ($y = 60x$), this time introducing tables. Students should recognize that the lines in the table correspond to the points they traced on the graph in Calculator Activity 6.

Lesson 8
Moving Toward a Car, Part 2

1. Here is the graph from Lesson 5 that shows a woman's distance from a car as a function of time.

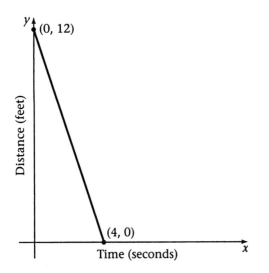

Which of these tables is a good match for the graph? Explain why you chose that table.

Table A

Time (seconds)	Distance (feet)
0	12
1	10
2	8
3	6
4	0

Table B

Time (seconds)	Distance (feet)
0	12
1	9
2	6
3	3
4	0

Table C

Time (seconds)	Distance (feet)
0	12
1	8
2	4
3	0
4	0

2. Choose the sentence that matches this table.

   A. A horse walked away from a stable at a rate of 6 feet per second.

   B. A horse was 42 feet away from a stable and walked toward it at a rate of 7 feet per second.

   C. A horse was 42 feet away from a stable and walked toward it at a rate of 6 feet per second.

   D. A horse walked away from a stable at a rate of 7 feet per second.

Time (seconds)	Distance (feet)
0	42
1	35
2	28
3	21
4	14
5	7
6	0

3. For each incorrect answer in Question 2, make a table that could correspond to it.

     A Visual Approach to Functions / © 2002 Key Curriculum Press

TEACHER NOTES

Students have been working with points on a graph, and now they see those ordered pairs arranged in a table. This lesson ties tables to sentences and graphs. The first scenario is a familiar one from Lesson 5.

Answers

1. Table B is the correct one. Students should note that it is the only table where the rate of walking is constant. The other tables will not produce straight lines.

2. Sentence B

3. Sentence A

Time (seconds)	Distance (feet)
0	0
1	6
2	12
3	18

Sentence C

Time (seconds)	Distance (feet)
0	42
1	36
2	30
3	24

Sentence D

Time (seconds)	Distance (feet)
0	0
1	7
2	14
3	21

 Extension: See Calculator Activity 8 _____

Here we use the graphing calculator to connect the equation, the table, and the graph to set up Lessons 9–13.

Answers to Calculator Activity

1. They are always the same. Points match entries in the table.

2. $y = 42 - 7x$. Answers should include a sentence describing how they found the equation.

Lesson 9
Putting It All Together

1. Here is a graph that shows a surfer's distance from the shore as a function of time, for several seconds. The table of values that goes with the graph is also shown.

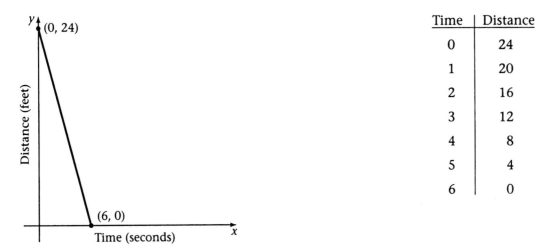

Time	Distance
0	24
1	20
2	16
3	12
4	8
5	4
6	0

Which of the following equations matches the graph and table? Explain why you chose that equation.

A. $y = 24x - 6$ C. $y = 4x + 24$

B. $y = 24 - 6x$ D. $y = 24 - 4x$

2. Now let's look at the graph and table for a different function.

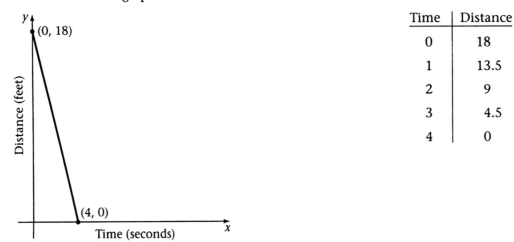

Time	Distance
0	18
1	13.5
2	9
3	4.5
4	0

a. Which equation matches the graph and table?

A. $y = 18x - 4$ C. $y = 4.5x + 18$

B. $y = 18 - 4.5x$ D. $y = 18 - 4x$

b. Does each pair of values in the table satisfy the equation you chose?

      A Visual Approach to Functions / © 2002 Key Curriculum Press

TEACHER NOTES

Students will use equations, graphs, and tables for a function throughout their mathematical careers. We want them to realize that all three represent the same thing. Discuss what would happen if the graph/function continued. Would it make sense? Would speed continue to be 6 feet per second past $x = 6$? Should the graph stop? This is a good time to discuss other quadrants.

For extra practice, and to tie the lesson together, you may wish to revisit Question 2 from Lesson 8. In that lesson, students connected the tables with sentences for the horse walking toward the stable. Have them match each of those situations to its equation below:

$$y = 42 - 6x \text{ (Sentence C)}$$

$$y = 42 - 7x \text{ (Sentence B)}$$

$$y = 6x \text{ (Sentence A)}$$

$$y = 7x \text{ (Sentence D)}$$

Answers

1. Equation D; each ordered pair must fit the equation.

2. a. B

   b. Yes

 Extension: See Calculator Activity 9 _____

Answers to Calculator Activity

1. $y = 42 - 6x$

2. $y = 22 - 6x$

3. The lines are parallel. The entries in both tables decrease by 6 feet each second (or y-coordinates are always 20 units apart). Neither surfer will pass the other.

4. The y-intercept is the same, but the slope of Y2 is steeper than the slope of Y1, so the surfer is moving faster. The entry for $x = 0$ is the same for Y1 and Y2, but after that, Y2 descends at a faster rate. This surfer was 42 feet away from the shore and surfing toward it at 7 feet per second.

5. $y = 12 - 3x$ and $y = 12 - 4x$ have the same y-intercept and starting distance. $y = 12 - 3x$ and $y = 10 - 3x$ have the same speed and the graphs are parallel.

Lesson 10
On a Bike

George rode his bike from the basketball court at the speed of 5 feet per second.

1. Fill in the table below giving George's distance from the court after each second. Continue for 12 seconds.

Time (seconds)	Distance (feet)
0	
1	

2. How far is George from the court after 4 seconds? After 4.5 seconds?

3. When is George 15 feet from the court? When is he 17.5 feet from the court?

4. Write an equation for George's distance from the court as a function of time. Use y for his distance in feet and x for the number of seconds elapsed.

5. What do you think the graph will look like? Draw a sketch.

6. Graph the table values you found in Question 1. (Scale your axes.) This should match the graph of the equation. Was your sketch right?

7. In terms of George's bike ride, what does the slope represent?

8. In terms of George's bike ride, what would an increase in the y-intercept mean? How about a sharper upward slope? How about a gentler slope?

Brainstorm ways to write a formula from the table of values before students do Question 4.

Students will almost certainly use different scales for their graphs. They should not confuse the different looks of their graphs with slopes that are actually different, which Question 8 refers to.

Answers

1.

Time (seconds)	Distance (feet)
0	0
1	5
2	10
3	15
4	20

2. He is 20 feet away after 4 seconds.
   He is 22.5 feet away after 4.5 seconds.

3. He is 15 feet away after 3 seconds.
   He is 17.5 feet away after 3.5 seconds.

4. The equation is $y = 5x$.

5–6.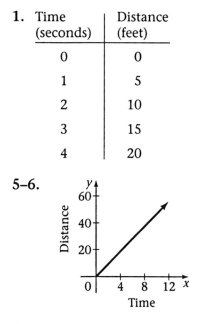

7. The slope of the graph represents the rate of riding and also shows up as the coefficient of x in $y = 5x$.

8. An increase in the y-intercept would mean he starts off farther from the court. A sharper slope indicates he's riding faster, and a gentler slope indicates he's riding slower. (This is true as long as the the scale has not changed—it is always possible to to play with scales and make lines with the same slope look very different.)

Extension: See Calculator Activity 10 _____

Answers to Calculator Activity

1. They are the same.

2. **a.** The graph starts higher up and is steeper. The table entries for y start higher and increase more quickly. He started farther away from the court and rode faster.

   b. The y-intercept is 7. It is where the graph crosses the y-axis, where the entry for x is 0, and what you get if you plug in 0 for x in the equation.

Lesson 11

The Boat Ride

Susan and Niki were in a pedal boat 35 feet from a dock. They pedaled toward it at a steady rate of 3.5 feet per second.

1. Fill in the table below giving their distance from the dock after each second. Continue until they reach the dock.

Time (seconds)	Distance (feet)
0	
1	

2. How long does it take Susan and Niki to reach the dock?

3. Write an equation for their distance from the dock (call it y) in terms of the number of seconds that have passed (use x for the number of seconds).

4. Graph the relationship you found in Question 3.

5. What does the y-intercept on your graph represent? What does the x-intercept represent? What does the slope represent?

6. If the y-intercept were higher, what would this tell you about Susan and Niki's boat ride? What if there were a sharper downward slope? A gentler slope?

    A Visual Approach to Functions / © 2002 Key Curriculum Press

For Question 3, a common mistake students make is to write $y = 3.5x$. Suggest that students choose lines from the table to check their formula.

Once again, you may want to discuss the meaning of going past 0 into other quadrants and whether or not it would make sense in this context.

Answers

1.

Time (seconds)	Distance (feet)
0	35
1	31.5
2	28
3	24.5
4	21
5	17.5
6	14
7	10.5
8	7
9	3.5
10	0

2. It takes Susan and Niki 10 seconds to reach the dock.

3. $y = 35 - 3.5x$

4.

5. The y-intercept represents where they start, or how far they are from the dock initially. The x-intercept represents how long it takes them to reach the dock. The slope represents their pedaling speed.

6. An increase in the y-intercept would mean they started farther away. A sharper slope would mean they pedaled faster, and a gentler slope would mean they pedaled more slowly.

Extension: See Calculator Activity 11

Answers to Calculator Activity

1. $y = 35 - 3.5x$; Answers will vary. Possible window: [0, 10, 1, 0, 35, 5].

2. $y = 45 - 3.5x$; Parallel, but higher up.

Lesson 12

Chasing a Ball

Jamila is standing 4 feet from a merry-go-round. She runs away from it chasing her ball across the park at the rate of 3 feet per second.

Her distance from the merry-go-round depends on the amount of time that has gone by. So, her distance is a function of time. You can represent a function by a table of values, a graph, or an equation.

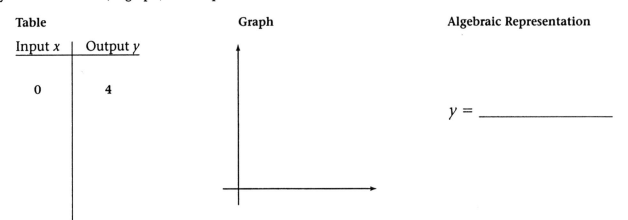

Table		Graph	Algebraic Representation
Input x	Output y		
0	4		$y = $ _____

1. The first line of the table is filled in. Fill in the rest of the table. Pick a line in the table and use it to write a sentence about Jamila.

2. In the space provided, graph your function. What is a good choice for the range of x if you want to look at the first 10 seconds? What about the range of y? Explain how to choose a good scale for your graph.

3. Write the equation for Jamila's distance from the merry-go-round over time. Enter your function into your calculator and graph it. What does x represent? What does y represent?

4. The point (5, 19) is on the line. Using this information, write a sentence about Jamila.

5. How far is Jamila from the merry-go-round after 8 seconds?

6. After how many seconds is she 75 feet from the merry-go-round?

7. Find the answer to Question 6 by solving the equation.

8. Use a graphing calculator to find the answer to Question 6: Graph $Y_1 = 4 + 3x$ and $Y_2 = 75$. Use $\boxed{\text{TRACE}}$ to find the coordinates of the point where the two lines cross. Did you get the same answer as in Questions 6 and 7? Why do you suppose this method works?

9. Suppose Jamila started off 5 feet farther away from the merry-go-round. How would the graph change? Suppose she ran faster by 2 feet per second. How would the graph change?

A Visual Approach to Functions / © 2002 Key Curriculum Press

TEACHER NOTES

This lesson ties together an equation, a graph, and a table as conveying the same information. Students solve a problem using all three tools. They also study and interpret points in all three formats.

Question 7 asks students to solve an equation. Question 8 introduces a different method for solving the equation: finding the point where the graph of the function crosses the graph of the solution. Students trace to find where $y = 4 + 3x$ crosses the constant function $y = 75$. You may ask students to think about how this corresponds to solving a single equation and use the connection to talk about the transitive property or substitution.

Answers

1. | Input x | Output y |
    |:---:|:---:|
    | 0 | 4 |
    | 1 | 7 |
    | 2 | 10 |
    | 3 | 13 |
    | 4 | 16 |
    | 5 | 19 |

    A possible sentence is "After 3 seconds Jamila was 13 feet away from the merry-go-round."

2. The range for x can be 0 to 10. The y-range could be 0 to 40 as $y = 34$ when $x = 10$. A good scale will make the best use of the space available for the graph.

    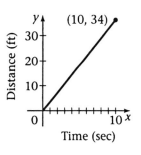

3. $y = 4 + 3x$, where x is time in seconds and y is distance in feet.

4. After 5 seconds Jamila is 19 feet from the merry-go-round.

5. After 8 seconds Jamila is 28 feet from the merry-go-round.

6. After 23.67 seconds she is 75 feet from the merry-go-round. (Depending on the method they use, students may give a more approximate answer.)

7. Change y to 75 in the equation and solve for x; $x = 23.67$.

8. Tracing also gives $x = 23.67$. The answer is the same no matter how you solve the problem. Students may give different explanations as to why this method works.

9. If she started 5 feet farther from the merry-go-round, the y-intercept would be 9 rather than 4. If her pace was 2 feet per second faster, the slope would be 5, not 3.

Extension: See Calculator Activity 12 _____

Answers to Calculator Activity

1. In 1 hour, it will be 1,004 miles away. In 2 hours, it will be 1,576 miles away. The equation is $y = 432 + 572x$; x represents how much time has passed, and y represents how far the plane is from New York.

2. Answers will vary. Possible window: [0, 5, 1, 400, 2400, 100].

3. Answers will vary. Sample sentence: "After 2.6 hours the plane will be 1,919.2 miles from New York."

4. After 2.74 hours. You can find this answer by solving the equation, by tracing on a graph, or by looking at a calculator table.

Lesson 13

Distance After x Amount of Time

1. A cargo plane is 20 miles from an airfield. It is approaching the airfield at a rate of 240 miles per hour, or 4 miles per minute. You want a linear equation giving the distance from the airfield in miles, y, as a function of time elapsed in minutes, x. Which is the correct way to write this?

   A. $y = 20x + 4$

   B. $y = 20 + 4x$

   C. $y = 4 - 20x$

   D. $y = 20 - 4x$

   For each incorrect answer, write a sentence which could correspond to the equation.

2. Jeri and June rowed their boat away from the shore at a steady pace. After 5 seconds they were 20 feet away. You want to write a linear equation giving the distance from the shore in feet, y, as a function of time elapsed in seconds, x, since they began rowing. Which is the correct way to write this?

   A. $y = 20 + 5x$

   B. $y = 4x$

   C. $y = 5x$

   D. $y = 20 - 5x$

   For each incorrect answer, write a sentence which could correspond to the equation.

3. A hot-air balloon takes off 2 miles inland from the coast. A steady breeze is blowing it further inland. After 4 hours it is 12 miles away from the coast. You want to write a linear equation giving the distance in miles, y, from the coast over time elapsed in hours, x. Which is the correct way to write this?

   A. $y = 2 + 3x$

   B. $y = 2 + 2.5x$

   C. $y = 12 + 2x$

   D. $y = 4 + 6x$

   For each incorrect answer, write a sentence which could correspond to the equation.

4. Explain why there is no "12" in the correct answer to Question 3, even though it is part of the information given in the problem.

5. Notice that the equation can always be written "Distance after x amount of time = initial distance + or − rate of motion times x." Does this formula work for all the problems you have done so far? Give examples. When is it "+" and when is it "−"? Explain why.

   A Visual Approach to Functions / © 2002 Key Curriculum Press

TEACHER NOTES

You may use this lesson as an assessment or as further practice writing linear equations from word problems. The reinforcement will make it clear that there is a pattern to the equations. The last question points out the formula and asks students to think about positive and negative values for the rate.

In Question 1, the rate is given, but in Questions 2 and 3, students must figure out the rate before they can choose the correct answer. Question 3 is a little difficult since the slope is not an integer.

Answers

1. D. Possible sentences for equations A, B, and C:

    A. A plane was 4 miles away from an airfield and was moving away from it at a rate of 20 miles per minute.

    B. A plane started off 20 miles away from an airfield and was moving away from it at a rate of 4 miles per minute.

    C. A plane started off 4 miles away from an airfield and was moving toward it at a rate of 20 miles per minute.

2. B. Possible sentences for equations A, C, and D:

    A. They were 20 feet away from the shore and were moving away from it at a rate of 5 feet per second.

    C. They started at the shore and moved away from it at a rate of 5 feet per second.

    D. They were 20 feet away from the shore and were moving toward it at a rate of 5 feet per second.

3. B. Possible sentences for equations A, C, and D:

    A. The balloon takes off 2 miles away from the coast and is moving away from it at a rate of 3 miles per hour.

    C. The balloon takes off 12 miles away from the coast and is moving away from it at a rate of 2 miles per hour.

    D. The balloon takes off 4 miles away from the coast and is moving away from it at a rate of 6 miles per hour.

4. Even though you don't see a "12" in the equation, plugging in 4 for *x* would give 12 for *y* in equation B.

5. Examples will vary. It is a "+" if you are moving away from an object and distance is increasing. It is a "−" if you are moving toward the object and distance is decreasing. The formula always works, but sometimes the rate of motion is not given and must be calculated; sometimes the initial distance equals zero and therefore does not show up in the equation, for example, $y = 5x$.

Extension: Calculator Activity 13 (Teacher-led)

Students practice coming up with an equation given a graph or two lines from a table (for example, two points). (Note: This extension can be done with the class as a whole using an overhead graphing calculator or using a sketch on the overhead projector if an overhead calculator is not available.)

Finding the Equation

1. Enter $Y_1 = 14 - 2x$ into a graphing calculator in such a way that the class cannot see it. Set the initial value for the table at 0 and the interval as 1. Show the class the graph and the table. (Note: Do not use TRACE because then the equation appears on the graph.)

   Work with the class on how to get the equation with this information. Ask students to come up with a distance versus time sentence to which it could correspond.

2. Do a few more examples like this: $Y_1 = 7 + 2.5x$; $Y_1 = 10 - 4x$. You can also let a student come up and enter an equation for the class to guess. Positive y-intercepts will work best in terms of applications students have seen so far.

3. For an extra challenge, change the interval on the table to 2. This will make it harder for students to obtain the slope, but you can ask them to deduce the rate of motion in units per second after figuring out the distance traveled in 2 seconds. Use other interval values if the above gives the class no trouble. After each equation has been obtained, remember to have the students come up with an application.

Lesson 14
Graphing Functions That Change

Functions are useful in computer programming. For example, if you were writing a computer game and you wanted to show four monkeys moving around in a cage, you could use a function for each monkey's position.

1. Suppose the graphs below show each monkey's distance from the front of the cage in feet as a function of time in seconds. Describe each monkey's movement as completely as you can. Include the rate, or speed, for each segment of the graph. Compare the movements of the different monkeys.

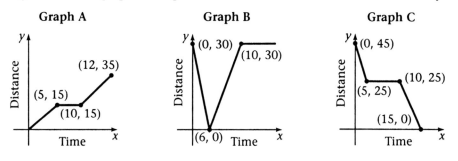

Graph A   Graph B   Graph C

a. Graph A:

b. Graph B:

c. Graph C:

2. Sketch the graph of a distance and time function that could match each monkey's movement. Put in coordinates for all the important points on the graph.

   a. The first monkey was 10 feet from the front of the cage, moved 3 feet closer to the front in 3 seconds, stood for 2 seconds, and then walked back to its original spot in 2 seconds.

   b. The second monkey ran away from the front of the cage at 5 feet per second for 4 seconds, stopped for 5 seconds, then went back to the front of the cage at 5 feet per second.

   c. The third monkey moved away from the front of the cage at 3 feet per second for 4 seconds. It stopped for another 4 seconds, then walked away at the rate of 5 feet per second for 1 second.

TEACHER NOTES

Piecewise functions are usually considered an advanced topic, but are useful in modeling real-life situations. Discuss "piecewise" before this lesson. Here, students are not yet using equations, but they are given enough information to draw the graph (times, distances, rates). The extension will set up Lesson 15, where equations are given for each segment.

Answers

1. Graph A: The monkey is at the front of the cage and walks away from it at the rate of 3 feet per second. It is 15 feet away after 5 seconds and stands still for 5 seconds. Then it continues to walk away at a rate of 10 feet per second for 2 seconds. After 12 seconds it is 35 feet away from the front of the cage.

   Graph B: The monkey is 30 feet from the front of the cage. It walks toward the front of the cage at the rate of 5 feet per second, reaching it after 6 seconds. It goes back to 30 feet away moving at a rate of 7.5 feet per second. After 4 more seconds it is again 30 feet away and now stops.

   Graph C: The monkey is 45 feet from the front of its cage. It walks toward the front at the rate of 4 feet per second for 5 seconds and stops for 5 seconds. It then takes 5 more seconds to reach the front, moving at a rate of 5 feet per second and reaching the front after 15 seconds total.

2. a.

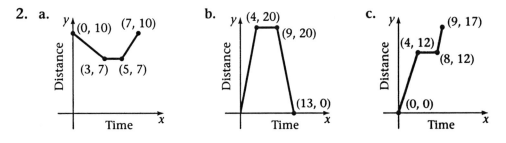

Extension: See Calculator Activity 14 _____

Answers to Calculator Activity

1. Yes

2. The graph is stretched out vertically and 10 times taller. This monkey moves 10 times faster and 10 times farther than the first monkey.

3. The graph is 10 times bigger but has the same shape as the first graph. The monkey moves 10 times farther but takes 10 times as long, so it moves at the same speed as the first monkey.

Lesson 15

Finding the Right Functions

In Lesson 14, you drew graphs of piecewise functions. Here you will look at those functions and find their equations.

Choose the set of functions that matches each situation. Explain why the other two sets are incorrect. For each incorrect set, graph the function and make up a situation to which it could correspond. Be sure your situation matches the appropriate rates and times.

1. Jack was standing 10 feet from the tree, walked 3 feet toward the tree in 3 seconds, stood for 2 seconds, and then walked back to his original spot in 2 seconds.

Function A	Function B	Function C
$y = 10 - x$ for $0 \le x \le 3$	$y = 10 - 3x$ for $0 \le x \le 3$	$y = 10$ for $0 \le x \le 3$
$y = 7$ for $3 < x \le 5$	$y = 1$ for $3 < x \le 5$	$y = 3x + 1$ for $3 < x \le 5$
$y = \left(-\frac{1}{2}\right) + \left(\frac{3}{2}\right)x$ for $5 < x \le 7$	$y = 1 + \left(\frac{9}{2}\right)(x - 5)$ for $5 < x \le 7$	$y = 31 - 3x$ for $5 < x \le 7$

2. Jamie ran away from the tree at 5 feet per second for 4 seconds, caught her breath for 5 seconds, then went back to the tree moving at 4 feet per second.

Function A	Function B	Function C
$y = 5x$ for $0 \le x \le 4$	$y = 5x$ for $0 \le x \le 4$	$y = 5 + 4x$ for $0 \le x \le 4$
$y = 20$ for $4 < x \le 5$	$y = 20$ for $4 < x \le 9$	$y = 21$ for $4 < x \le 9$
$y = 20 - 4x$ for $5 < x \le 10$	$y = 56 - 4x$ for $9 < x \le 14$	$y = 57 - 4x$ for $9 < x \le 14$

3. Jorge walked away from the tree at 3 feet per second and stopped to wave to a friend after 4 seconds. After another 4 seconds, he continued to walk away at 5 feet per second.

Function A	Function B	Function C
$y = 3x$ for $0 \le x \le 4$	$y = 3x$ for $0 \le x \le 4$	$y = 3x$ for $0 \le x \le 4$
$y = 12$ for $4 < x \le 8$	$y = 12$ for $4 < x \le 8$	$y = 12$ for $4 < x \le 8$
$y = 12 + 5x$ for $8 < x$	$y = 52 - 5x$ for $8 < x$	$y = 5x - 28$ for $8 < x$

4. Look at all the piecewise functions in Questions 1–3. Find the two piecewise functions that are not connected. Can you use these functions to describe a person's motion? Explain.

Here we introduce equations for piecewise functions. Students may need a reminder of what the different inequality symbols mean.

Answers

1. Function A. The graph for Function B has the person walk 9 feet, rather than 3 feet, toward the tree, and the graph for Function C has the person first stay in place, then walk farther away from the tree.

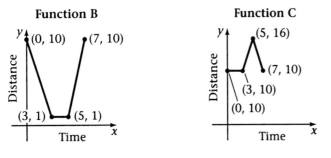

   (Situations will vary.)

2. Function B. The graph for Function A is disconnected. The third piece starts at (5, 0) rather than at (5, 20). The graph for Function C is connected, but the initial piece indicates the person was 5 feet away to start with and moved away at 4 feet per second.

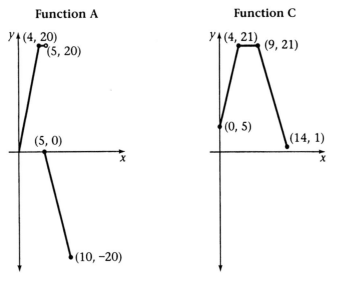

   (Situations will vary.)

3. Function C. Function A is not correct as the last piece begins at (8, 52) rather than at (8, 12). According to Function B, the person walks back to the tree rather than continuing on after the 4-second pause.

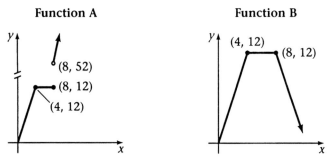

Function A

Function B

(Situations will vary.)

4. Function A in Question 2 and Function A in Question 3 are not connected. No, a person cannot go from one distance to another in zero amount of time.

Lesson 16
Graph Medley

1. Choose the graph of distance as a function of time that matches each situation.

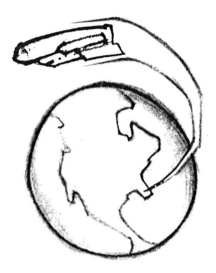

   A. Riding a Ferris wheel (the rider's distance from the ground):

   B. Running sprints back-and-forth (the distance from the starting point):

   C. Earth and Sun (Earth's distance from Sun):

   D. Space shuttle flight (the space shuttle's distance from Earth):

   E. Riding an elevator to the top floor, stopping at each floor (the rider's distance from the ground):

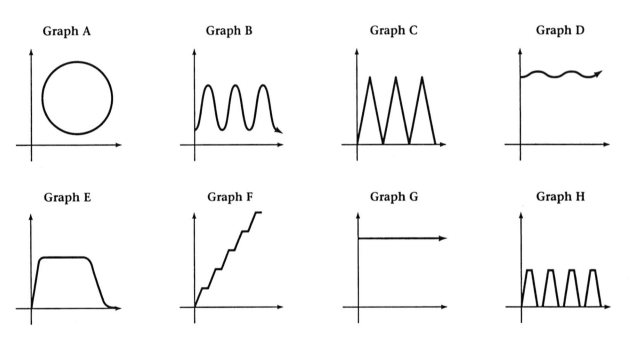

2. Which graph cannot be a graph of distance as a function of time? Explain why.

3. For each graph you did not choose, describe the motion and give a situation that matches the graph.

TEACHER NOTES

This lesson challenges students to apply what they have learned about the shape of graphs to some new applications. You can use it for review, as a quiz, or as a challenge.

Students may not know the path of the space shuttle: it lifts off like a rocket, stays in orbit for several days, and then lands like an airplane. Students with English as a Second Language (ESL) may also need some explanation of *Ferris wheel* and *sprints*.

For an extra challenge, have students also choose a graph of speed as a function of time for each situation.

(*Answers to challenge:* 1. F or H   2. D or I   3. E or H   4. F   5. I)

Answers

1. **A.** Graph B

    B. Graph C (or Graph H, if they assume resting between sprints)

    C. Graph D (or Graph G, if they assume a perfectly circular orbit)

    D. Graph E

    E. Graph F

2. Graph A is impossible, since it is not a function. A graph of distance and time cannot circle back on itself, since it is not possible to be two places at one time.

3. Graph H (or Graph C): The answer should describe a back and forth or up and down motion.

    Graph G: The answer should describe a situation in which distance remains constant.

    Graph D: The answer should describe a situation in which distance varies only slightly with time.

    Graph A: No situation matches this graph. See Question 2.

Calculator Activity 1: Walking with a Motion Detector

Using a motion detector and a graphing calculator, make graphs of your own distance from an object over time. The object can be a door, a wall, or any other surface that the motion detector can be pointed directly toward. You can also place the motion detector on a table, facing you as you walk.

1. With a classmate, take turns walking in front of the motion detector and looking at the resulting graphs. How many different kinds of graphs can you make with your own walking motion?

2. Choose a classmate to walk forward and backward in front of the detector. Turn your back so you can't see where your classmate is walking. Can you tell where your classmate is just by looking at the graph? Can you tell whether your classmate is closer or farther from the detector? Can you tell whether your classmate is walking quickly, slowly, or stopped altogether?

3. Take turns between doing the walking and the guessing. Practice this until you can describe your classmate's walk just by looking at the graph.

 Calculator Activity 2: Walking with a Motion Detector, Part 2

1. Look at the graphs in Lesson 2. Try to produce each of those graphs using a motion detector. Choose five graphs and write down instructions for producing them with a motion detector.

2. How do you produce a horizontal line using the motion detector? How do you produce a vertical line?

Calculator Activity 3: Comparing Graphs

Enter each equation into the graphing calculator, then look at its graph. Write a story or situation to match each graph of distance and time.

1. $y = 1.5$

2. $y = 2$ and $y = 2x$ (Imagine these are distance and time graphs for two people or things. Think of a story or situation for these two graphs.)

3. $y = 1.5x$ and $y = 10 - 2x$

4. $y = 3 - x$ and $y = 2 - 0.5x$

5. $y = x^2$ and $y = 10 - x^2$

```
█████ FORMAT
Xmin=0
Xmax=10
Xscl=1
Ymin=0
Ymax=10
Yscl=1
```

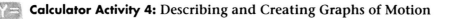

Calculator Activity 4: Describing and Creating Graphs of Motion

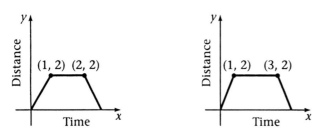

1. Describe some things that are alike about the two graphs above. Describe some things that are different.

2. Using the motion detector, try to produce two graphs exactly like the ones above. Write down exact instructions that a classmate could follow to produce each graph with a motion detector.

Calculator Activity 5: The Beetle and the Lettuce

A beetle starts crawling toward a piece of lettuce. The beetle's distance from the lettuce (in centimeters) is given by the equation $y = 20 - 0.5x$. Enter this equation into the graphing calculator.

1. According to the graph, how far away from the lettuce does the beetle start out? What are the coordinates of this point on the graph?

2. Use $\boxed{\text{TRACE}}$ to find at least three other sets of coordinates for the beetle's position. For each set, write a complete sentence describing the beetle's distance from the lettuce and the time.

3. How long does it take the beetle to reach the lettuce? Explain how you can tell this just by looking at the graph. What are the coordinates of the point that shows the beetle reaching the food?

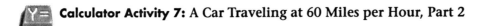

Calculator Activity 6: A Car Traveling at 60 Miles per Hour

Enter the equation $y = 60x$ into the graphing calculator and look at its graph. Suppose that the graph shows distance and time for a car traveling from home. Time is measured in hours and distance in miles.

1. Use ⎣TRACE⎦ to look for the points where $x = 1$, $x = 2$, and $x = 3$. Write sentences about the car's distance and time at those three points.

2. Could you get those same three points by using the equation? Explain.

3. How many miles is the car traveling each hour?

4. What is the car's speed? How can you tell?

5. Find the car's distance and write sentences for the points where $x = 3.5$, $x = 4.5$, $x = 8.2$, and $x = 9.25$. Convert these decimals to hours and minutes (0.5 is 30 minutes, etc.), and use hours, minutes, and miles in your sentences.

6. Could you get those same three points by using the equation? Explain.

Calculator Activity 7: A Car Traveling at 60 Miles per Hour, Part 2

1. What is the equation that gives distance traveled in miles for a car moving at 60 miles per hour?

2. Enter the equation $y = 60x$ into the graphing calculator and then look at the table for this equation. Choose three lines in the table and write sentences about distance and time at these points.

3. Change the x-interval for the table to 0.1. Find the lines in the table where $x = 3.5$, $x = 4.5$, and $x = 8.2$. Write a sentence for each line. Convert the decimals to minutes and use hours, minutes, and miles in your sentences.

4. How does this relate to the graph you traced in Calculator Activity 6?

Calculator Activity 8: The Graph-Table Connection

1. Put the calculator in G-T (or Graphing-Table) mode. Enter the equation $y = 12 - 3x$. What is the connection between this equation and the table you chose in Question 1 from Lesson 8? Use ⎣TRACE⎦ to locate points on the graph. Do they match the entries in the table?

2. Write an equation that would match the table and the sentence in Question 2 from Lesson 8. Enter it into your calculator and check the graph and the table to see if they match Question 2. Write down your equation and explain how you found it.

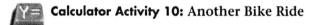 **Calculator Activity 9:** Two Surfers

1. Write an equation for a surfer who was 42 feet away from the shore and surfing toward the shore at a rate of 6 feet per second. Graph this as your first equation.

2. At the same time, another surfer started out 22 feet away from the shore and surfed toward the shore at a rate of 6 feet per second. Graph this as your second equation.

3. Compare the two graphs. What do you notice? Compare the tables. What do you notice? When will one surfer pass the other?

4. Now clear your second equation and graph the equation $y = 42 - 7x$. What do you notice about the two graphs? What do you notice about the tables? Write a sentence explaining what you know about this surfer.

5. Compare these equations: $y = 12 - 3x$, $y = 10 - 3x$, and $y = 12 - 4x$. Which ones have the same y-intercept? Which ones are parallel? Which ones have the same starting distance? Which ones have the same speed?

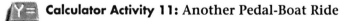 **Calculator Activity 10:** Another Bike Ride

Put your graphing calculator in G-T mode.

1. Enter $Y_1 = 5x$. This was the equation for George's bike ride. What relationships do you see between the equation, the graph, and the table?

2. On a different day, the equation for George's bike ride was $y = 8x + 7$. Enter this equation for Y_2 into your calculator.

   a. How is the graph different from the first one? How is the table different from the first one? How was George's bike ride different on this day?

   b. What is the y-intercept for this graph? How do you find it on the graph? How do you find it in the table? How do you find it using the equation?

Calculator Activity 11: Another Pedal-Boat Ride

1. Susan and Niki were 35 feet from the dock and pedaling toward it steadily at a rate of 3.5 feet per second. Enter the equation for Susan and Niki's distance from the dock. What is a good window setting for viewing your graph?

2. On a different day, Susan and Niki started out 10 feet farther away from the dock but pedaled at the same rate. What is the equation for this boat ride? Enter the equation into your calculator. How does this graph compare to the graph from Question 1?

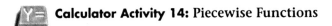

Calculator Activity 12: Flight from New York

A plane is 432 miles from New York. It is now traveling away from New York at the rate of 572 miles per hour. Its distance from New York (in miles) is a function of time from now (in hours) and its speed is constant, so the graph is linear.

1. How far will the plane be from New York in 1 hour? 2 hours? Write the equation for the plane's distance from New York as a function of time, starting now. What does *x* represent? What does *y* represent?

2. Enter the equation into your graphing calculator. What is a good window for viewing the graph?

3. Trace to a point on your graph and write a sentence about the plane using the coordinates.

4. When will the plane be 2000 miles from New York? List all the different ways you can find this answer.

Calculator Activity 14: Piecewise Functions

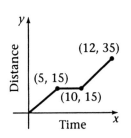

1. Graph this piecewise function. The main points are (0, 0), (5, 15), (10, 15), and (12, 35). Enter all the *x*-values into list L1: 0, 5, 10, 12. Enter all the *y*-values into list L2: 0, 15, 15, 35. Does your graph match the first graph in Lesson 14?

2. Go back to the list and multiply every coordinate in list L2 by 10. How does your graph look now? If this is the function for another monkey moving around in a video game, describe the monkey's movements.

3. What if you also multiply list L1 by 10? How does your graph look different now? Describe the monkey's movements if they match this function.

A Visual Approach to Functions / © 2002 Key Curriculum Press

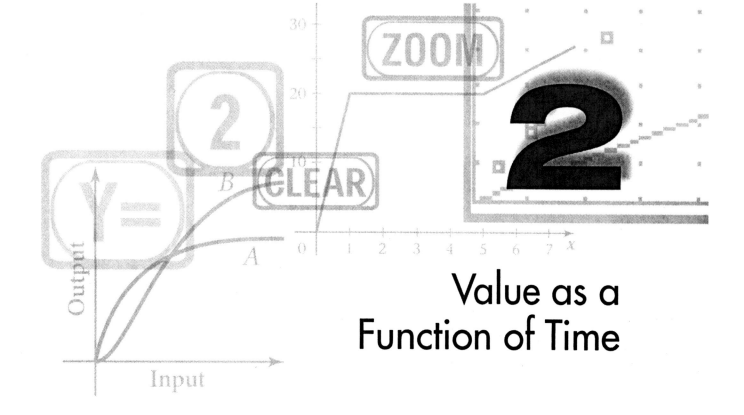

Value as a Function of Time

This chapter focuses on functions that model the value of
an object over time. As they did in Chapter 1, students
begin by looking at qualitative graphs and studying what
the shapes of the graphs mean. They then move on
to quantitative graphs and investigate the coordinates
related to points on the graphs. Finally they work with
tables and equations.

Even students in advanced mathematics classes often
have trouble looking at a function and deciding
whether a particular interval is increasing or decreasing.
Keep in mind that students should be able to look at
a graph out of context and decide whether it depicts
an increasing or decreasing function.

Lesson 1

Increasing and Decreasing Values

1. Each sentence describes the value of an object over time. Choose the graph that matches the description.

    a. The value of the autographed book decreased at first, and then increased as the star became popular again.

    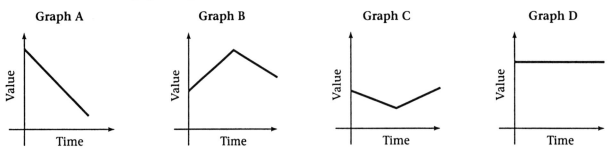

    b. The value of the company's stock first increased and then decreased.

    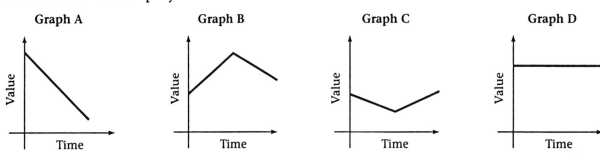

    c. The value of Jake's land decreased and then remained the same.

    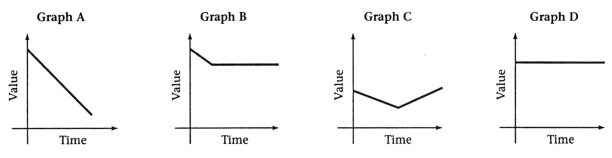

2. For each graph you did not choose in Question 1, write a sentence to describe what is happening.

A Visual Approach to Functions / © 2002 Key Curriculum Press

TEACHER NOTES

This lesson reviews the graphical representation of a function. In this chapter, the application is value as a function of time. This lesson is similar to the first lesson in Chapter 1. If students have done a selection of lessons in that chapter, this lesson should give them no problems.

Remind students that "value over time" can also be called "value versus time" or "value as a function of time." You may wish to discuss variables as quantities that take on different values and the importance of graphs for conveying this changing information. Here time is the independent variable, and value is the dependent variable, since it depends on, or varies with, time.

Remind students that as time goes by, you move to the right on the graph and that value increases as you move up on the graph.

Answers

1. **a.** Graph C   **b.** Graph B   **c.** Graph B

2. **a.** Graph A: The value of the book decreased over time.

   Graph B: The value of the book first increased, then decreased.

   Graph D: The value of the book stayed the same over time.

   b. Graph A: The value of the stock decreased over time.

   Graph C: The value of the stock first decreased, then increased.

   Graph D: The value of the stock stayed the same over time.

   c. Graph A: The value of Jake's land decreased over time.

   Graph C: The value of Jake's land first decreased, then increased.

   Graph D: The value of Jake's land stayed the same over time.

Extension: See Calculator Activity 1 _____

Students are asked to write their own equations for increasing, decreasing, and constant value. Although this may be a challenge for them, being able to use trial and error on a graphing calculator will help.

Answers to Calculator Activity

1. **a.** This graph is a horizontal line with y-intercept at $(0, 2)$.

   b. This graph has a y-intercept at $(0, 0)$ and a rate of change of 1.

   c. This graph has a y-intercept at $(0, 3)$ and a rate of change of -1.

2. **a.** $Y_2 = x$

   b. $Y_3 = 3 - x$

   c. $Y_1 = 2$

Comparing Values

1. The value of Lynn's house first decreased, then remained the same. Finally, the value began to increase.

   a. Decide which of these graphs best shows the value of Lynn's house.

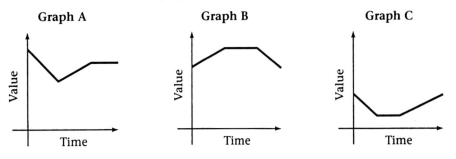

   Graph A   Graph B   Graph C

   b. For each graph you did not choose, write a sentence that would fit the graph.

2. Each graph below shows how two different cars are changing in value as time passes.

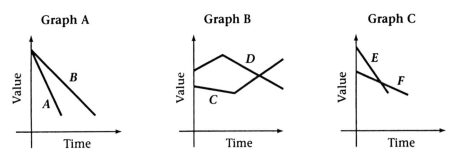

   Graph A   Graph B   Graph C

   a. For each graph, describe the value of each car. In your description, be sure to include comparisons of the two cars.

   Graph A:

   Graph B:

   Graph C:

   b. For each graph, decide which car you would prefer to own. Then explain your decision.

A Visual Approach to Functions / © 2002 Key Curriculum Press

TEACHER NOTES

In this lesson, students continue investigating the value of an object over time. Discuss depreciation if the word is unfamiliar to students. Depreciation is a real-world application, one that affects everyone sooner or later. Students may find this especially interesting if they are buying their first car or if they already own one. In Question 2, students explore the value of two objects on the same graph. They may find it helpful to discuss an example of this beforehand.

Answers

1. a. Graph C

    b. Graph A: The value of the house first decreased, then increased slowly, but not back to the original level. Finally, it stayed constant.

    Graph B: The value of the house first increased, then remained the same for a period of time. Finally, the value decreased.

2. a. Graph A: The cars are purchased for the same amount. Car B depreciates more slowly than car A.

    Graph B: Car D is purchased for a higher price. Car D appreciates at first, then depreciates at about the same rate. Car C decreases in value slowly and then increases in value at a faster rate. In the end, car C is worth more than car D.

    Graph C: Here both cars decrease in value. The more expensive car (car E) depreciates at a faster rate.

    b. Car B is a better value than car A. Over time, car C is a better value than car D and car F is a better value than car E.

Extension: See Calculator Activity 2

This activity helps students grasp the idea that the coefficient of x affects whether the graph is increasing or decreasing.

Answers to Calculator Activity

1. Y1 cost more, but decreased in value faster than Y2.
2. Y1 cost more than Y2, but decreased in value. Y2 slowly increased in value.
3. Answers will vary. The sign of the coefficient of the x-variable makes the function increase or decrease.

Lesson 3
Rates of Change

1. Jeremy, Sean, and Maria each purchased cars at the same time. Jeremy's car depreciated at a steady rate. Sean's car first depreciated quickly and then more slowly. At first, Maria's car depreciated slowly and then more rapidly. Decide which graph best shows the value of each car. Write each person's name next to the correct graph. Equal time intervals have been marked to help you decide.

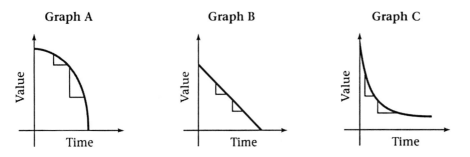

2. Each set of pictures shows Jack's reaction to the change in value of his property. For each set, sketch a graph to summarize the pictures. Then describe the change in value over time.

   a. Jack jumps for joy when the value of his baseball card collection increases, but feels terrible when it decreases.

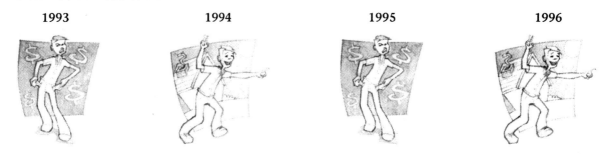

1993   1994   1995   1996

   b. Jack has bought stock in his favorite company. He feels triumphant when the value of the stock increases, but very worried when it decreases.

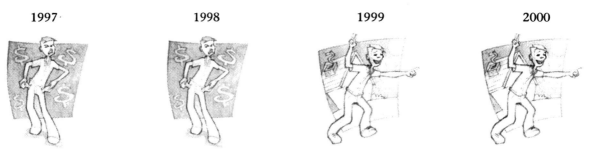

1997   1998   1999   2000

A Visual Approach to Functions / © 2002 Key Curriculum Press

TEACHER NOTES

This lesson reinforces what students learned in the two previous lessons of this chapter.

In Question 1, students compare changing rates of depreciation. Understanding decreasing and increasing rates of change is important in calculus and physics.

For Question 2, you may tell students to use straight lines or curved lines.

Answers

1. Graph A: Maria's car; Graph B: Jeremy's car; Graph C: Sean's car

2. **a.** The value of the baseball card collection first decreases, then increases, then decreases, and finally, increases.

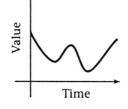

   b. Jack's stock loses value in '97 and '98, but then starts to increase in '99.

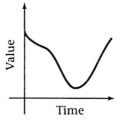

⌨ *Extension: See Calculator Activity 3* _____

In this activity, students will be entering equations to obtain separate graphs. For each graph, ask whether the graph shows decrease at a steady rate, decrease with an increasing rate of change, or decrease with a decreasing rate of change.

Answers to Calculator Activity

1. **a.** Y_1 shows a decrease at a steady rate; Y_2 shows a decrease with an increasing rate of change; Y_3 shows a decrease with a decreasing rate of change.

2. **a.** Y_1 shows an increase at a steady rate; Y_2 shows an increase with an increasing rate of change; Y_3 shows an increase with a decreasing rate of change.

Lesson 4

Depreciation of a Car

1. The following graph shows the
    value of a car since it was purchased.
    Time (in years) is graphed along
    the *x*-axis, and the price (in dollars)
    is graphed along the *y*-axis. Decide
    which sentence is a good match for
    the graph.

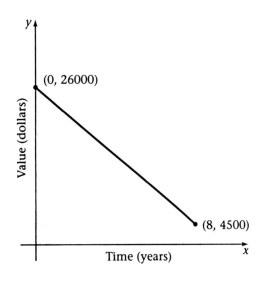

A. Harriet bought a car for $26,000. Its value decreased by $4,500 each year
   for 8 years.

B. Juan bought a car for $26,000. After 8 years it was worth $4,500.

C. Jason bought a car for $30,500. After 8 years it was worth $4,500.

D. Linda bought a car for $4,500. After 8 years it was worth $26,000.

2. Consider Sentence A. What was the car worth after 1 year? What would be
    the coordinates on the corresponding graph?

3. For each sentence you did not choose in Question 1, draw a graph that
    corresponds to it.

                                             A Visual Approach to Functions / © 2002 Key Curriculum Press

TEACHER NOTES

In the first three lessons of this chapter, students explored the value of an object over time using qualitative graphs, or graph sketches. Here, students are introduced to coordinates and they look at quantitative graphs.

With coordinates, students can calculate rates of change. You will be able to look at each graph more closely and ask the students how much each car depreciated each year.

In the answer to Question 3, the graph of A goes into negative values. Discuss with students how realistic this is.

Answers

1. Sentence B

2. The car was worth $21,500. The point on the graph is (1, 21500).

3. A.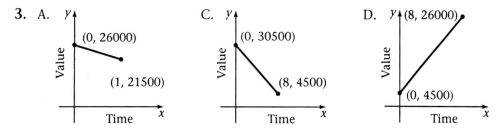

 Extension: See Calculator Activity 4 _____

Students use the [TRACE] key to come up with statements about the value of several cars over time. See if the students pick up on the fact that two of the cars are decreasing at the same rate.

Answers to Calculator Activity

1. Students may prefer the first car (because it costs less and holds its value better) or the last car (because it is worth more . . . but only for the first two years).

2. To find the annual rate of decrease, compare the y-intercept and the value after the first year. Students may also refer to the number in front of x in the equation.

Lesson 5

Value as a Function of Time

1. Think of things you own or things you might buy. The graphs show the value of an object as a function of time. Choose something whose value could match each graph. Explain why it is a good match, giving as many details as you can. You can choose the units for time. Include the rate of decrease or increase per unit of time.

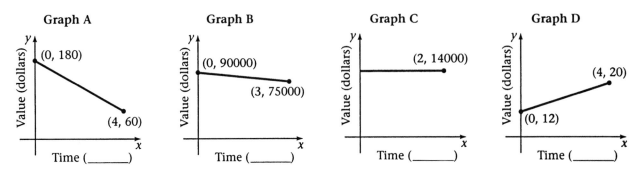

a. Graph A:

b. Graph B:

c. Graph C:

d. Graph D:

2. Each sentence describes the value of an object over time. Draw a graph to match each sentence. On your graph, put in the coordinates for the information given in the sentence.

    a. Anna purchased a set of tools for $4,500. Its value did not change.

    b. Jay bought a TV for $500. It depreciated at a steady rate, and after 3 years it was worth $350.

    c. Lorraine paid $12,000 for her motorcycle. It depreciated at a steady rate. It was worth $9,000 after 2 years.

     A Visual Approach to Functions / © 2002 Key Curriculum Press

TEACHER NOTES

This lesson continues the investigation of the value of an object over time. In Question 1, students choose objects to match graph scenarios. In the second question, they create graphs from descriptions. Students may need assistance in determining the scales to use. Often each axis requires a different scale. You might want to model a situation and discuss appropriate scales.

Answers

1. **a.** The initial value of the object was $180 and decreased $30 per year, to $60 after 4 years. Sample answer: television.

    b. The initial value of the object was $90,000 and decreased $5,000 per year, to $75,000 after 3 years. Sample answer: house.

    c. The value of the object remains constant over 2 years at $14,000. Sample answer: motorcycle.

    d. The initial value of the object was $12 and increased $2 per year, to $20 after 4 years. Sample answer: baseball card.

2. **a.**   **b.**   **c.**

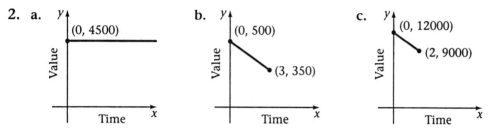

 Extension: See Calculator Activity 5 _____

Students use two data points to graph a line. It may be challenging for them to recognize that the first sentence provides the two data points they need. They can also find the rate of depreciation by comparing these points or by tracing the line over a 1-year interval.

Answers to Calculator Activity

1.

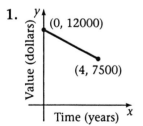

2. The rate of depreciation is $1,125 per year. The total amount of depreciation divided by the number of years gives the rate of depreciation per year.

Lesson 6

The Value of a Painting

Abe bought a painting from his friend Caroline for $1,350. Over the next 5 years, as Caroline became more famous, the painting's value increased steadily by $2,000 a year.

1. Fill in the table below with the painting's value for each year since it was purchased.

Time (years)	Value (dollars)
0	
1	

2. How much is the painting worth after 2 years? After $2\frac{1}{2}$ years?

3. When is the painting worth around $10,000?

4. How long does it take for the painting to increase $3,000 in value?

5. Write an equation for the value of the painting in terms of the number of years since it was purchased. Let y represent the value and x represent time.

6. Graph the relationship you found in Question 5.

7. For your graph, what does the y-intercept represent? What does the slope represent?

     A Visual Approach to Functions / © 2002 Key Curriculum Press

TEACHER NOTES

In this lesson, students create both the equation and the table. At this point, they should have a good sense of what the slope and intercepts mean in terms of the application.

You may want to use this lesson to explore input-output tables. Tell students that "$f(x)$" is the same as "y" in a function. That is, the ordered pair (x, y) can also be represented as $(x, f(x))$. Or each y-coordinate is determined by the corresponding x-value.

Question 6 is a good opportunity to discuss the importance of appropriate scales.

Answers

1.

Time (years)	Value (dollars)
0	1,350
1	3,350
2	5,350
3	7,350
4	9,350
5	11,350

2. The painting is worth $5,350 after 2 years and $6,350 after $2\frac{1}{2}$ years.

3. The painting is worth $10,000 after a little less than $4\frac{1}{2}$ years.

4. It takes $1\frac{1}{2}$ years for the painting to increase $3,000 in value.

5. The formula for the value of the painting is $y = 1350 + 2000x$.

6.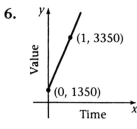

7. The y-intercept represents the initial value. The slope gives the increase in dollars per year.

Extension: See Calculator Activity 6

Students explore a situation similar to the one in the lesson. They interpret the meaning of a line in the table and a point on the graph.

Answers to Calculator Activity

1. a. $y = 170{,}000 + 3{,}000x$; sentences will vary depending on the points the students choose.

    b. Sentences will vary depending on the points the students choose. Sample answer: After 10 years the house will be worth $200,000, an increase of $30,000.

    c. Sentences will vary depending on the points the students choose.

Lesson 7

Analyzing a Depreciation Function

Kyle bought a boat for $26,000. Every year, its value decreases by $3,000. The value of the boat is a function of time.

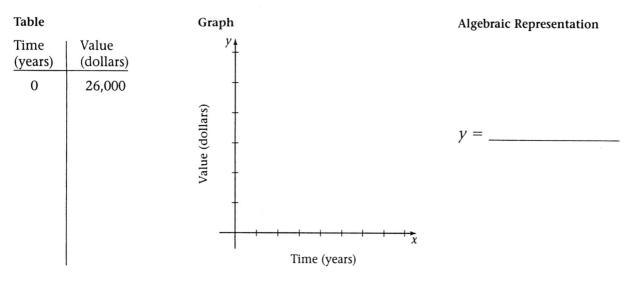

Table

Time (years)	Value (dollars)
0	26,000

Graph

Algebraic Representation

$y = $ _____

1. Complete the table giving the value of Kyle's boat for each year since he purchased it.

2. Graph the function, assuming Kyle's boat will last for 8 years. What is a good scale for the x-axis? What is a good scale for the y-axis? Explain why you chose each scale.

3. Write the equation that describes the boat's value over time. What does x represent? What does y represent?

4. If the boat was worth $3,000 more to start with, what would be the effect on the line? What would be the effect on the equation?

5. If the boat dropped in value $1,000 per year rather than $3,000 per year, what would be the effect on the line? What would be the effect on the equation?

Here students are asked to produce the table, the graph, and the equation of a function.

Answers

1–2. A good scale for the *x*-axis is 1-year intervals. A good scale for *y* is intervals of $5,000 (answers may vary from $2,000 to $10,000).

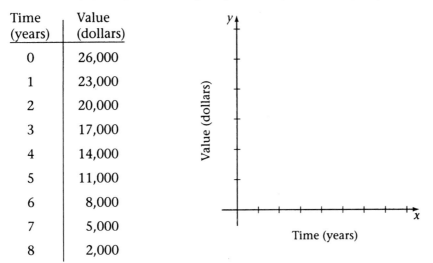

Time (years)	Value (dollars)
0	26,000
1	23,000
2	20,000
3	17,000
4	14,000
5	11,000
6	8,000
7	5,000
8	2,000

3. $y = 26,000 - 3,000x$; *x* represents time elapsed in years and *y* represents the value of the car in dollars.

4. The *y*-intercept would be 3,000 units higher, and the 26,000 in the equation would become 29,000.

5. The slope would be descending less steeply, and the 3,000 in the equation would become 1,000.

Extension: See Calculator Activity 7 _____

The focus of this activity is for students to begin with an equation, table, sentence, or graph describing a situation and to find the other three. You may want to provide other situations for them to investigate.

Answers to Calculator Activity

Answers will vary. Sample answer: Joan purchased her car for $45,000. The car depreciates $3,500 every year. The equation for this situation is $y = 45,000 - 3,500x$.

Lesson 8

Finding the Right Equation

1. Bill owns a flower stand. He started his business for $8,000, but as he gets more and more customers, the value of his business grows by $7,000 each year.

   a. Choose the equation that describes the value of his business, y, as a function of the number of years, x.

      A. $y = 15,000 + x$

      B. $y = 15,000x$

      C. $y = 8,000x + 7,000$

      D. $y = 8,000 + 7,000x$

   b. For each of the equations you didn't choose, write a sentence to go with it.

2. Jack and Amelia bought a boat for $12,500. After 2 years it is worth $10,000.

   a. Choose the equation that describes the value of their boat assuming a constant depreciation.

      A. $y = 12,500 - 2,000x$

      B. $y = 10,000 + 1,250x$

      C. $y = 12,500 - 1,250x$

      D. $y = 10,000 + 2x$

   b. For each of the equations you didn't choose, write a sentence to go with it.

3. Five years ago, Sid paid $2,300 for a necklace. Its value has not changed. Which equation describes the value of the necklace over time?

      A. $y = 2,300 + x$

      B. $y = 2,300 - x$

      C. $y = 2,300$

      D. $y = 2,300x$

TEACHER NOTES

In this lesson, students work on finding the right equation for different situations.

Answers

1. **a.** Equation D

   b. Answers should include

   A. A starting value of $15,000 and an increase of $1 per year.

   B. A starting value of $0 and an increase of $15,000 per year.

   C. A starting value of $7,000 and an increase of $8,000 per year.

2. **a.** Equation C

   b. Answers should include

   A. It costs $12,500 and decreases in value by $2,000 per year.

   B. It costs $10,000 and increases in value by $1,250 per year.

   D. It costs $10,000 and increases in value by $2 per year.

3. Equation C

Extension: See Calculator Activity 8

Students create a table and a graph for each equation presented in the lesson.

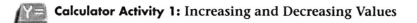

Chapter 2 | Calculator Activities

Calculator Activity 1: Increasing and Decreasing Values

1. Enter each equation into a graphing calculator. Look at the graph for each and write a sentence describing it.

    a. $Y_1 = 2$

    b. $Y_2 = x$

    c. $Y_3 = 3 - x$

2. Identify which of the equations above match each of these situations.

    a. a steady increase in value

    b. a steady decrease in value

    c. value staying constant

Calculator Activity 2: Comparing Values

1. Graph the equations $Y_1 = 3 - x$ and $Y_2 = 2 - 0.5x$. These functions show the value of two objects over time. Choose two objects to which these graphs could apply. Compare the value of the two objects.

2. Repeat Question 1 using the equations: $Y_1 = 3 - 0.8x$ and $Y_2 = 2 + 0.2x$.

3. Write three different equations that show decreasing value. Write three different equations that show increasing value. What part of the equation makes the function increase or decrease?

Calculator Activity 3: Rates of Change

1. Graph $Y_1 = 10 - x$, $Y_2 = 10 - 0.1x^2$, and $Y_3 = 0.1(x - 10)^2$. Set the window for both x and y from 0 to 10. Look at one graph at a time by turning off the other two graphs.

    a. Which graph shows decrease at a steady rate? Decrease with an increasing rate of change? Decrease with a decreasing rate of change? Explain.

    b. For each graph, write a story that matches the graph.

2. Repeat Question 1 for the equations $Y_1 = x$, $Y_2 = 0.1x^2$, and $Y_3 = -0.1(x - 10)^2 + 10$.

Calculator Activity 4: Depreciation of a Car

1. Graph $Y_1 = 27{,}000 - 1{,}000x$; $Y_2 = 27{,}000 - 2{,}000x$; and $Y_3 = 30{,}000 - 3{,}000x$. Set the window value for x from 0 to 10 and for y from 0 to 30,000. Let each graph represent the value of a car over time. Which car would you rather own? Why?

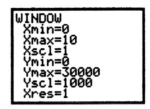

```
WINDOW
 Xmin=0
 Xmax=10
 Xscl=1
 Ymin=0
 Ymax=30000
 Yscl=1000
 Xres=1
```

2. Press TRACE to find the original price of each car and the annual rate of decrease. Explain how you found your answers.

3. Choose an object you own. Write down its original value and, assuming a steady rate of depreciation, decide the rate of decrease per year. Then graph the value over time.

   a. What does the y-intercept represent?

   b. What does the x-intercept represent?

 Calculator Activity 5: Value as a Function of Time

1. Rico bought a motorcycle for $12,000. Four years later, he was able to sell it for $7,500. Enter these two points into lists in your calculator. Enter time (number of years) into list L1, and value (in dollars) into list L2. Then plot the points using Stat Plot and Zoom Stat. Now have the calculator draw a line through the points using linReg and vars. Copy the graph here:

2. What was the rate of depreciation for Rico's motorcycle? Explain how you find depreciation.

Calculator Activity 6: The Value of a House

1. Gayle and Jerry bought a house for $170,000. Its value increased $3,000 per year.

   a. Write an equation for the value of the house in terms of the number of years.

   b. Enter the equation into your calculator. Use the Table function and look at the table for the equation. Pick a line in the table and write a statement about the house at that point.

   c. Graph the line. Press TRACE to pick out a point. Write a sentence about the house at that point.

 Calculator Activity 7: Choosing Your Own Function

Think of a situation involving the value of an object over time. Write an equation that matches the situation.

1. Draw a graph of this equation. Label the starting value.

2. Make a table of values for the first five years.

3. Enter the equation into your calculator. Check the graph and table to see if they match.

 Calculator Activity 8: Comparing the Table and Graph

For each of the equations given in the lesson, use your calculator to create the table and graph. Then write a sentence comparing each table with its graph.

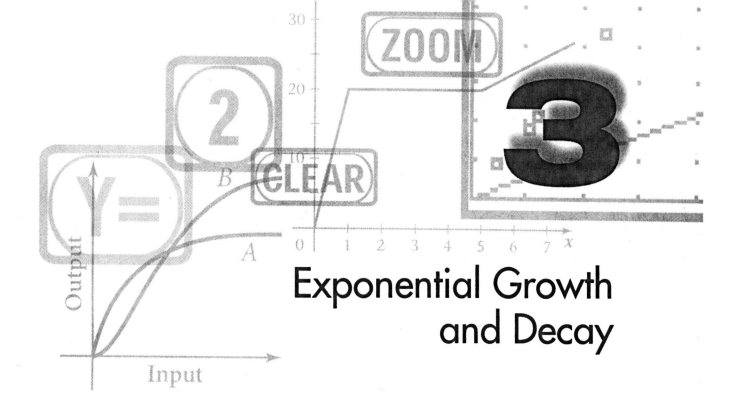

Exponential Growth and Decay

This chapter introduces students to exponential functions. The lessons use population growth, investment returns, and radioactive decay to demonstrate exponential growth and decay. Students begin by studying qualitative graphs. Next they move on to quantitative graphs. Toward the end of the chapter, tables and equations are introduced.

The functions are introduced through the concepts of doubling, tripling, and halving. This chapter also lays the foundation for in-depth investigation of nonlinear functions in Chapters 4–6.

Lesson 1

Population Growth

1. Population usually grows at an exponential rate. This is because the amount of increase is proportional to the number of people present. Let's say the rate of growth for a town is 10% every 20 years. If the population is 100,000 people, 10% growth means an increase of 10,000 people over 20 years. But over the next 20 years after that, the population will grow by 10% of 110,000 people, or an increase of 11,000 people.

    The population of Francis's hometown is growing at an exponential rate. Which of the following graphs best represents the population over time?

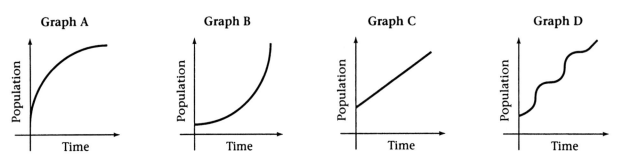

2. Over the last 10 years, the population where Ricky lives increased exponentially, but then leveled off due to overcrowding. Which of the following graphs best represents the population over time?

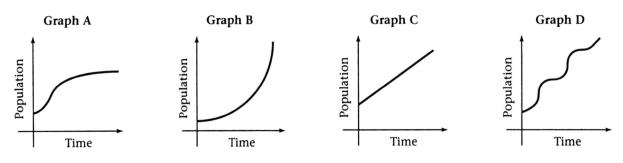

A Visual Approach to Functions / © 2002 Key Curriculum Press

TEACHER NOTES

The focus of this lesson is qualitative graphs of exponential growth. Exponential functions may be new to students, as algebra usually focuses on linear functions. To clarify the distinction for your students, you might have them do some investigations. For example, have them enter 100,000 into a calculator to represent a population, and then repeatedly add 10%. They will see an increasing rate of growth, which can also be seen in the graphs of exponential growth functions. They may also be able to think of times when they heard of something "growing exponentially."

The questions use the term "proportional to," which may be confusing to students. You might want to discuss this with them before they answer the questions.

For Question 1, students may find it beneficial to discuss that, whereas the slope of the curve is not a constant, the time it takes for a population to double, called "doubling time," is fixed. For instance, with the example above, they might expect a population of 100,000 growing by 10% annually to double after 10 years. In fact, it doubles every 7 years or so. Suggest to students that they mark the point on each curve where the original population has doubled and then compare the two points.

Answers

1. Graph B

2. Graph A

Extension: See Calculator Activity 1 _____

Students use Stat Plot to compare linear growth with exponential growth.

Answers to Calculator Activity

2. Both graphs start at the same initial position. Graph A increases at a constant rate. Graph B also increases, but has an increasing rate of change.

3. Graph B is more likely to represent the population of a town, because it grows at an exponential rate.

Lesson 2

Populations and Investments

1. Each graph shows the population over time for two cities. For each graph, compare the initial population and the rate of growth.

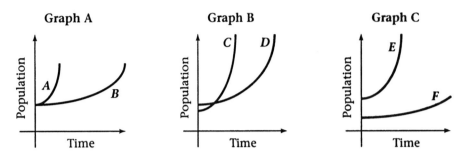

2. When you invest money at a fixed percentage rate, it increases in the same way that population does. This means that the more money there is in the account, the faster it grows.

   Imagine that the graphs in Question 1 represent the amount of money over time. For each graph, compare the amounts invested and decide which is the better investment.

3. When the population of an area grows and then levels off due to overcrowding, the population where it levels off is called the "saturation level."

   Each of these graphs shows the population over time for two towns. For each graph, compare the population present at the beginning and the saturation level.

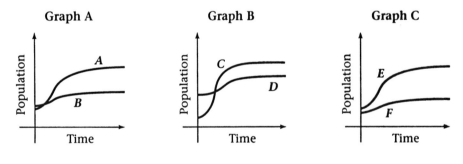

TEACHER NOTES

In this lesson, students continue to look at qualitative graphs of population. The concept is extended to money investments and their growth. You may want to discuss fixed percentage rates for investments with your students.

Answers

1. Graph A: Initially, the two populations are the same size, but *A* is increasing at a faster rate than *B*.

   Graph B: In the beginning, the population of *D* is larger, but *C* is increasing at a faster rate. The population of *C* soon surpasses that of *D*.

   Graph C: The initial population of *F* is less than the population of *E*. *F* grows at a slower rate. The population of *F* will always remain less than that of *E* as long as both continue to grow at the rates shown.

2. Graph A: *A* is the better investment.

   Graph B: *C* is the better investment.

   Graph C: *E* is the better investment, although you do need to have more money to start out with.

3. Graph A: Initially, the population of *A* is slightly less than the population of *B*. Then *A* increases at a more rapid rate and levels off later. The end population of *A* is larger than that of *B*.

   Graph B: At the start, *C* has the smaller population. It is about one-third the population of *D*. *C* increases at a more rapid rate and levels off later. The saturation level for C is higher than for D.

   Graph C: *F* has a smaller population in the beginning. It is about two-thirds the population of *E*. *E* increases at a more rapid rate than *F*. The saturation level of *E* is about twice that of *F*.

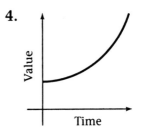 Extension: See Calculator Activity 2

Students use an imaginary bank account to investigate growth of an investment at a fixed APR. For Question 2, they may have to do a lot of trial and error to find that the number to multiply by must be greater than 1. In fact, it is 1.06, which gives the original number plus 6%. This idea will be useful in Chapter 4, when the students derive the formula for the new amount.

Answers to Calculator Activity

1. 10,600

2. 1.06

3. The graph will be curved upward like an increasing exponential function.

4.
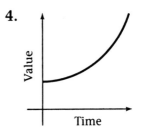

Lesson 3
Radioactive Decay

All radioactive elements decay over time (there are fewer and fewer atoms of the radioactive element as times goes by). Each has a different period of decay, called a "half-life." If you check back after one half-life, half of the atoms will have decayed into a nonradioactive substance. After another half-life, half of the remaining atoms will have decayed, and so on.

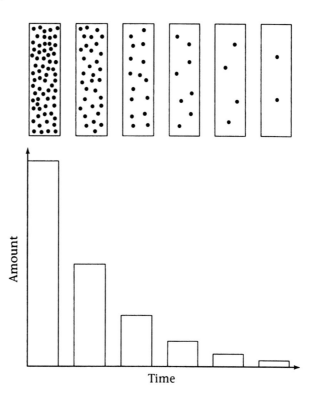

1. For a radioactive element, which of the following graphs best represents the amount present over time? (Hint: Mark off equal time intervals and compare the change in amount.)

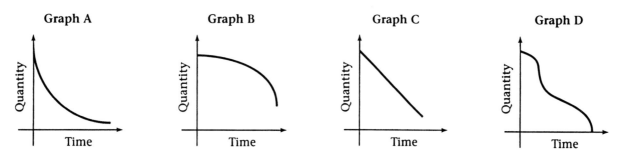

2. Each graph shows the decay of two radioactive elements. For each graph, compare the initial amounts present and the rate of decay.

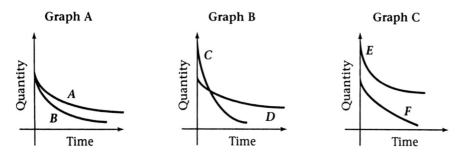

This lesson introduces the opposite of growth—decay. As a calculator activity, have students enter any number into the calculator and divide by 2 (or multiply by 0.5) repeatedly. First they will get half the original number, then one-fourth, and so on, but they will have a residual amount for a long time. (The calculator eventually rounds down to zero, but in reality the graph never reaches zero; there is just a very long "tail" on the graph.)

Answers

1. Graph A

2. Graph A: At the start there is the same amount of both substances. *B* decays at a faster rate than *A*, because it takes longer for half of *A* to disappear.

   Graph B: There is more of *C* at the beginning, but it decays at a faster rate than *D*.

   Graph C: Initially, there is more of *E*, and it decays at a slower rate.

Extension: See Calculator Activity 3

Students use Stat Plot to compare two different exponential decay functions.

Answers to Calculator Activity

1. c. The graph starts at an initial position of 100 and decreases exponentially, getting closer and closer to 0.

2. c. The graph starts at an initial position of 256 and decreases exponentially, getting closer and closer to 0.

3. Both graphs are decreasing exponentially at the same rate, but the second graph started at a higher initial position.

Lesson 4
Iodine-131

Radioactive iodine can be used to treat some kinds of cancer. A doctor is studying a sample of iodine-131, a radioactive substance. This graph shows the amount of iodine-131 over time.

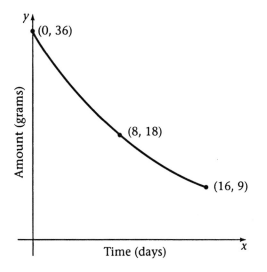

1. Decide which sentence is a good match for the graph.

   A. It took 9 days for 36 grams of the element to decay to 16 grams.

   B. The half-life of the element is 8 days.

   C. After 18 days, 36 grams of the element decayed to 8 grams.

   D. It took 8 days for 16 grams to decay to 9 grams.

2. a. How much iodine-131 did the doctor start with?

   b. How long did it take for that amount to be divided in half? That is, what is the half-life of iodine-131?

   c. After how many days will there be 4.5 grams left?

3. For each sentence you did not choose in Question 1, draw a graph that corresponds to it.

TEACHER NOTES

Students move from qualitative graphs to quantitative graphs of exponential decay. The focus of this lesson is to analyze actual *x*- and *y*-values on an exponential graph. Students identify the amount of a radioactive element at given times. They also determine the half-life.

Answers

1. Sentence B

2. **a.** There were 36 grams initially.

   b. It took 8 days for the amount to be halved.

   c. After 24 days there will be 4.5 grams left.

3.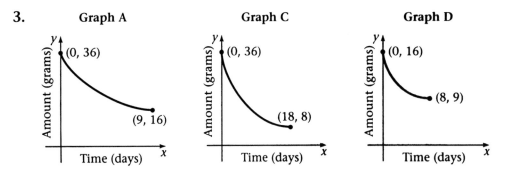

Extension: See Calculator Activity 4 _____

Answers to Calculator Activity

1. The initial amount is 48, and the half-life is 10.

2. The initial amount is 44, and the half-life is 12.

Lesson 5
Growth and Decay

1. Gardner invested $1,000 at a fixed percentage rate. After 12 years his investment doubled. Choose the graph that shows Gardner's investment.

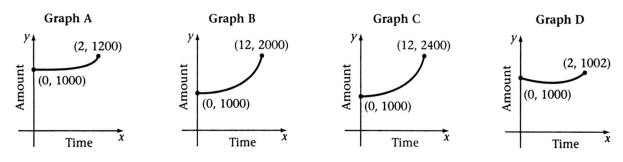

2. For each graph you did not choose in Question 1, write a sentence that describes it.

3. Twelve grams of a radioactive element decayed to 10 grams after 560 years. Choose the graph that best describes this.

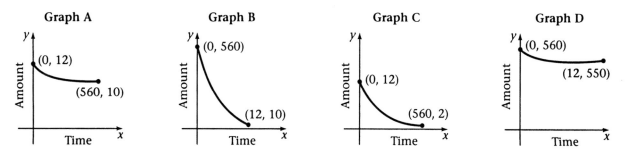

4. For each graph you did not choose in Question 3, write a sentence that describes it.

TEACHER NOTES

Students use clues from the graphs to choose the right exponential growth or decay function, and they write sentences to match the other choices.

Answers

1. Graph B

2. Answers may vary. Some examples include

    Graph A: Jackie invested $1,000. After 2 years she has $1,200.

    Graph C: Ms. Samuelson invested $1,000. Her investment is worth $2,400 after 12 years.

    Graph D: Jordan invested $1,000, and after 2 years the investment is worth $1,002.

3. Graph A

4. Answers may vary. Some examples include

    Graph B: After 12 years, 560 grams of a substance decayed to 10 grams.

    Graph C: Twelve grams of a substance decayed to 2 grams after 560 years.

    Graph D: After 12 years, 560 grams of a substance decayed to 550 grams.

Extension: See Calculator Activity 5

Before students complete the activity, you may want to model a similar problem. Students may benefit from seeing how to use the Calc menu to find the doubling rate.

Answers to Calculator Activity

1. a. The graph will show exponential growth.

    b. The doubling time is between 9 and 10 years.

2. a. You expect its y-intercept to be higher, but the rate of change is smaller, so that eventually the lower graph will cross it. The graph will show exponential growth.

    b. $y = 11,000 \cdot (1.07)^x$

    c. The graphs intersect at (10.25, 22001). This indicates the two investments are worth the same amount after 10 years 3 months.

Lesson 6

Investment Tables and Graphs

John invested $560 at a fixed percentage rate. After 10 years, his money had doubled.

1. Fill in the table below giving the amount of John's investment over 70 years.

Time (years)	Amount in Account (dollars)
0	560
10	
20	

2. How many decades will pass before John has $100,000?

3. Graph the first six points in the table above. Plan the scale for the *y*-axis before you plot the points. Draw a smooth curve to connect the points.

4. What does the *y*-intercept represent? Does the slope of the curve become steeper or gentler over time?

5. If the *y*-intercept were higher, what would that mean in terms of John's investment? What would it mean if the curve rose more steeply earlier on? How about a gentler rise?

6. The function for John's investment is $y = 560 \cdot 2^{(x/10)}$. Check to see that each point satisfies this equation.

Students continue to investigate exponential growth. The scenario is an investment at a fixed percentage rate. You may want to help students discover that the amount will always double after a fixed period of time. Question 6 brings home why these are called "exponential functions": writing the equation requires exponents.

Answers

1.

Time (years)	Amount in Account (dollars)
0	560
10	1,120
20	2,240
30	4,480
40	8,960
50	17,920
60	35,840
70	71,680

2. The amount would reach $100,000 after about $7\frac{1}{2}$ decades.

3.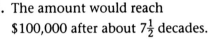

4. The y-intercept is the initial investment. The slope becomes steeper as time goes on. This is because the time it takes for John's money to double remains the same, but the amount that is doubled increases.

5. An increase in the y-intercept would mean a larger initial investment. If the curve rose more steeply earlier on, the doubling time would be shorter. A gentler rise would mean a longer doubling time.

6. Each point does satisfy the equation.

Extension: See Calculator Activity 6

Answers to Calculator Activity

1. The value after 1 year is $600.20. The value after 11 years should be double the amount after 1 year, $1200.40.

2. Because the doubling time is 10, you know that after 10 years there will be 1,120. You can simply double the 0–9 values to get the 10–19 values. 1 corresponds to 11 and so on.

3. The value after 53 years is 22,062. This can be done by doubling the value at 3 five times (or multiplying by 2^5).

Lesson 7

A Half-life Table

Jeanette is studying a substance that has a half-life of 20 years.

1. Fill in the table below giving the amount of the substance present over the next 120 years, in 20-year intervals.

Time Elapsed (years)	Substance Remaining (grams)
0	72
20	
40	

2. How many decades will pass before less than a gram of the substance is left?

3. Graph the first six points in the table. Before you plot the points, make sure to think of the scale for the y-axis. Then draw a smooth line to connect the points.

4. What does the y-intercept represent? Does the curve fall more steeply or more gently over time?

5. If the y-intercept were higher, what would that mean? What would it mean if the curve fell more steeply earlier on?

6. Check to see that each point satisfies the equation $y = 72 \cdot 2^{(-x/20)}$.

Students continue to focus on exponential decay. After completing a table describing the amount of a decaying substance over time, students graph the information. They may need help deciding which scale to use.

Answers

1.

Time Elapsed (years)	Substance Remaining (grams)
0	72
20	36
40	18
60	9
80	4.5
100	2.25
120	1.125

2. After 120 years, 1.125 grams will remain. After 140 years, only 0.5625 gram will remain. Thirteen decades will pass before there is less than a gram left.

3.

4. The y-intercept represents the initial amount present. The curve falls more gently over time.

5. An increase in the y-intercept means there is more of the substance initially. If the curve fell more steeply, it would mean the substance has a shorter half-life.

6. Each point does satisfy the equation.

Y= Extension: See Calculator Activity 7 _____

Answers to Calculator Activity

2. The amount left after 1 year is 69.5. The amount left after 21 years will be 34.8.

3. Yes, you can create the table by taking half of each entry.

4. The value after 53 years is 11.47. This solution can be found by cutting the value at 13 in half two times (multiplying by 2^{-2}).

Lesson 8

Exponential Equations

1. Edna and Saul invested $2,500. Their investment doubled every 12 years. Choose the equation that describes the investment. Let y represent an amount in dollars and x the time in years.

   A. $y = 2{,}500 \cdot 2^{(x/12)}$

   B. $y = 2{,}500 \cdot 2^x$

   C. $y = 12 \cdot 2^{(x/2500)}$

   D. $y = 2{,}500 \cdot 2^{(-x/12)}$

2. For each equation you did not choose in Question 1, write a sentence to go with it.

3. Twenty-four grams of a substance has a half-life of 16 hours. Choose the equation that gives the amount present over time.

   A. $y = 16 \cdot 2^{(-x/24)}$

   B. $y = 24 \cdot 2^{(-x/16)}$

   C. $y = 24 \cdot 2^{(x/16)}$

   D. $y = 16 \cdot 2^{(x/24)}$

4. For each equation you did not choose in Question 3, write a sentence to go with it.

5. The initial population of Alesha's hometown was 499. The population tripled every 5 years. Choose the equation that gives the population over time.

   A. $y = 499 \cdot 2^{(-x/5)}$

   B. $y = 499 \cdot 3^{(x/5)}$

   C. $y = 5 \cdot 3^{(x/499)}$

   D. $y = 5 \cdot 3^{(-x/499)}$

TEACHER NOTES

In this lesson, students identify equations representing exponential growth and decay. They should be making these connections: a positive exponent means exponential growth and a negative exponent means exponential decay; the coefficient is the initial amount; the denomination in the exponent is the doubling time or half-life. Students may want to use a calculator to check their answers.

Answers

1. Equation A

2. Answers will vary. Sample answers:

   B. The population starts at 2,500 and doubles every year.

   C. For a certain type of bacteria, the doubling time is 2,500 minutes. The population model starts with 12 million bacteria.

   D. The population is 2,500 at present, and we can expect it to cut in half every 12 years.

3. Equation B

4. Answers will vary. Sample answers:

   A. Sixteen grams of a substance is present, and the substance has a half-life of 24 years.

   C. The $24 million investment will double every 16 years.

   D. The $16 million investment will double every 24 years.

5. Equation B

 *Extension: See Calculator Activity 8*

Answers to Calculator Activity

1. The y-intercept is at 10, and the graph increases exponentially.

2. The amount doubles every time x increases by 12.

3. The amount doubles from $x = 1$ to $x = 13$.

4. It will double as long as the x-interval is 12.

 Calculator Activity 1: Using Lists

1. Use the List function to create two graphs. Use lists L1 and L2 to create Graph A, and use lists L1 and L3 to create Graph B.

   a. Enter numbers from 0 to 5 into list L1.

   b. Enter 100, 110, 120, 130, 140, and 150 into list L2.

   c. Enter 100, 110, 121, 133, 146, and 161 into list L3.

   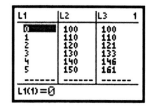

2. Compare the two graphs. Make as many observations and comparisons as you can.

3. Which graph is more likely to represent the population of a town? Why?

 Calculator Activity 2: Interest Rates

Imagine you have just put $10,000 in the bank at 6% fixed APR (annual percentage rate).

1. How much will you have in the bank 1 year from now?

2. What number can you multiply by 10,000 to give you the correct answer to Question 1?

3. Enter 10,000 into your calculator. Continue to multiply by the number you found in Question 2 until you have your account balance for the next 10 years. Predict what the graph of your account balance will look like.

4. Use List to graph your answer to Question 3. Sketch the graph here:

Calculator Activity 3: Radioactive Decay

1. Imagine you are studying a radioactive substance. Follow these steps to create a graph showing the decay.

    a. Enter numbers from 0 to 7 into list L1 and enter 100, 50, 25, 12.5, 6.25, 3.125, 1.5625, and 0.78125 into list L2.

    b. Now use Stat Plot and Zoom Stat to see the data graphed. Look at the unconnected as well as the connected version.

    c. Describe the graph.

2. Repeat Question 1. This time, enter 256, 128, 64, 32, 16, 8, 4, and 2 into list L3.

3. Compare the two graphs. Describe some differences and similarities between the two substances.

 Calculator Activity 4: Two Radioactive Substances

Nathan is studying two radioactive substances. Answer the following questions for the two substances.

1. Graph $Y_1 = 48(2^{-x/10})$ and find a good viewing window. Use [TRACE] to find the initial amount present and the half-life.

2. Turn off Y_1. Graph $Y_2 = 44(2^{-x/12})$. Use [TRACE] to find the initial amount present and the half-life.

 Calculator Activity 5: Doubling Time

1. James invested $10,000. The interest rate is 8% compounded annually.

    a. Graph $Y_1 = 10,000 \cdot (1.08)^x$.

    b. What is the doubling time?

2. Anna invested $11,000. The interest rate is 7% compounded annually.

    a. How do you think the graph of Anna's investment will compare to the graph of James's investment?

    b. Write the equation for Anna's investment. Then graph it.

    c. Where do the graphs intersect? What does this point tell you about the two investments?

Calculator Activity 6: Investment Tables and Graphs

The equation $Y_1 = 560 \cdot 2^{(x/10)}$ describes Jacob's investment.

1. Graph the equation. What is the value of the investment after 1 year? What do you expect the value to be after 11 years?

2. Check to see if you were right by using the Table function on your calculator. Look at the table for years 0 to 9. Can you create the table for years 10 to 19? How?

3. Try to predict the investment value after 53 years using only the entries for x-values from 0 to 9. Explain.

 Calculator Activity 7: More Radioactivity

The equation $Y_1 = 72 \cdot 2^{(-x/20)}$ shows the decay of substance D.

1. Graph the equation on a graphing calculator.

2. What is the amount left after 1 year? What do you expect the value to be after 21 years?

3. Check to see if you were right by using the Table function on your calculator. Look at the table for years 0 to 19. Can you create the table for years 20 to 39?

4. Try to predict the amount left after 53 years using only the entries for x-values from 0 to 19. Explain.

Calculator Activity 8: More Doubling Time

1. Enter $Y_1 = 10 \cdot 2^{(x/12)}$ into your calculator. Describe the curve.

2. What is the increase after 12 years? 24 years?

3. Compare the y-value at $x = 1$ and $x = 13$. What do you notice?

4. Do you think this will always be the case no matter which interval value you choose?

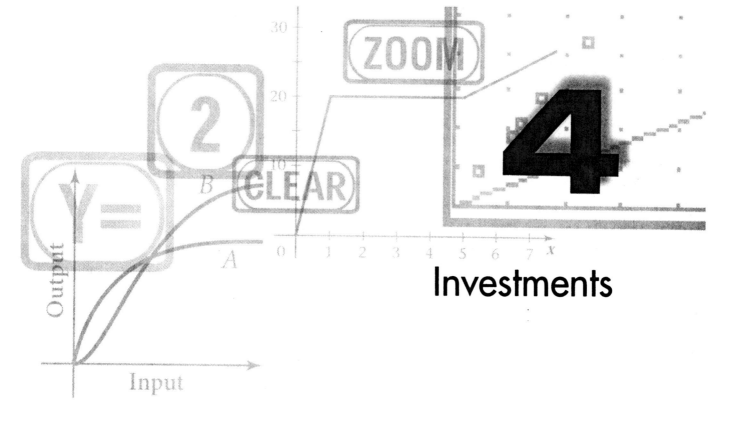

Investments

The focus of this chapter is the exponential growth of investments over time. As in the previous chapters, students look at qualitative graphs, then move on to quantitative graphs and tables. Throughout the chapter, they investigate interest rates that compound at different times (annually, semi-annually, quarterly, and daily). Starting with Lesson 4, they write equations for the account balance. Lessons 6 and 7 develop the general equation. In Lesson 8, students apply what they learned about functions describing exponential growth to a problem involving exponential decrease.

Lesson 1

Describing Investments

Investments grow at a rate that is proportional to the amount invested. When you graph the amount invested over time, the slope of the curve increases over time. However, the time it takes to double the amount is fixed.

1. Vincent made an investment that is growing as described above. Which of the following graphs best represents the dollar amount over time?

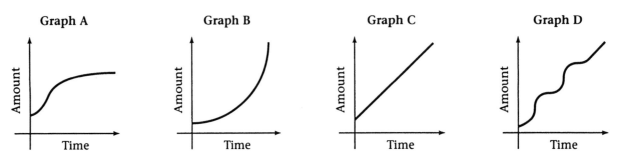

2. Two investments are growing at different rates. Each graph below shows the relationship between amounts invested and time elapsed for the two investments. For each graph, compare the initial amount invested and the rate of growth.

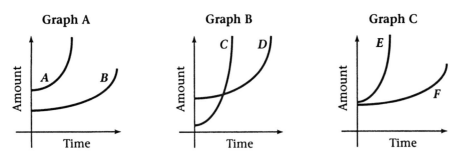

A Visual Approach to Functions / © 2002 Key Curriculum Press

You may want to present an example of a graph of an investment over time, as discussed in the lesson's introductory paragraph, before students complete the lesson. Students will benefit from a discussion and examples of investments, including the terms *principal, interest, fixed rate,* and *compounded annually.*

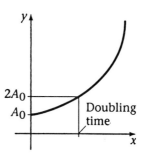

Answers

1. Graph B

2. Graph A: It looks as though *A* invested twice the money *B* did. *A*'s rate of growth is better, because the time it takes for the money to double is much shorter.

   Graph B: *C* invested about a quarter of the money *D* did, but *C*'s rate of growth is much faster.

   Graph C: *E* and *F* invested the same amount of money, but *E*'s rate of growth is much higher.

Extension: See Calculator Activity 1 _____

In this activity, students begin to investigate the doubling time for exponential functions.

Answers to Calculator Activity

1. **b.** Find the initial amount and then [TRACE] to find the time when that amount has doubled.

   c. After 14 years, the investment will be at $200.

   d. The amount will double at the 8-year mark.

2. **c.** After 14 years, the investment will be at $202. The investment will be at $200 after a little less than 14 years.

   d. The amount will double at the 9-year mark.

3. **c.** After 14 years, the investment will be at $112.25. The investment will be at $200 after 24 years.

   d. The amount will double at the 13-year mark.

4. The first and third functions start at the same amount, but the first function grows faster. The second function starts at a higher amount and grows faster than the third function, but slower than the first function.

Lesson 2

Interpreting Investment Graphs

Zack made an investment at a fixed interest rate compounded annually. The graph shows Zack's investment over time.

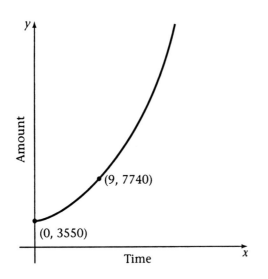

1. Decide which sentence is a good match for the graph.

   A. It took 9 years for the investment to double.

   B. The investment increased by $7,740 after 9 years.

   C. It took 9 years for the original investment of $3,550 to reach the sum of $7,740.

   D. $3,550 was invested at a 9% interest rate.

2. For each sentence you did not choose in Question 1, draw a graph that matches it. Be sure to put in the appropriate points.

A Visual Approach to Functions / © 2002 Key Curriculum Press

Students continue to investigate exponential growth by looking at problems involving investment over time.

Answers

1. Sentence C

2. Possible graphs for the other sentences are

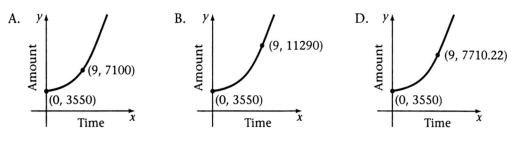

 ## Extension: See Calculator Activity 2 _____

Before beginning this activity, tell students they will look at investments given in terms of interest rates and figure out the doubling time, because banks give an annual interest rate rather than a doubling time.

Answers to Calculator Activity

2. All three graphs are increasing. It takes Hannah about 12 years to reach the doubling point. It takes Sara about 9 years and Jerome a little more than 7 years.

3. Doubling time for 4% is almost 18 years; for 12% it's slightly more than 6 years.

4. No

Lesson 3

Investment Tables

1. Yolanda invested $10,000 at a fixed percentage rate. She did not withdraw the principal or interest, and after 12 years the investment tripled. Choose the graph that shows Yolanda's investment.

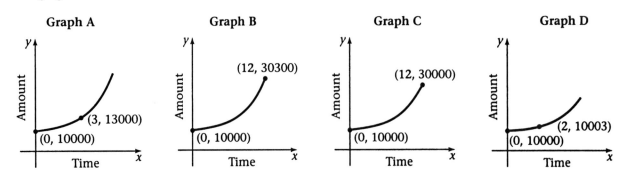

| Graph A | Graph B | Graph C | Graph D |

2. For each graph you did not choose in Question 1, write a sentence that matches the information in the graph.

3. Nelson invested $100 at 5% interest compounded annually. Which of the following data tables describes Nelson's investment?

	Table A			Table B			Table C	
Time (years)	Amount (dollars)		Time (years)	Amount (dollars)		Time (years)	Amount (dollars)	
0	100		0	100		0	100	
1	105		1	105.05		1	105	
2	110		2	110.10		2	110.25	
3	115		3	115.15		3	115.76	
4	120		4	120.20		4	121.55	

A Visual Approach to Functions / © 2002 Key Curriculum Press

TEACHER NOTES

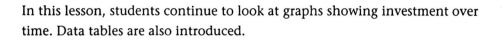

In this lesson, students continue to look at graphs showing investment over time. Data tables are also introduced.

Answers

1. Graph C

2. Graph A: Answers may vary. A possible sentence: An initial investment of $10,000 was made, and after 3 years the investment had grown to $13,000.

   Graph B: Answers may vary. A possible sentence: Jane made an initial investment of $10,000, and after 12 years the investment grew to $30,300.

   Graph D: Answers may vary. A possible sentence: An initial investment of $10,000 was made, and after 2 years the investment had grown to $10,003.

3. Table C

Extension: See Calculator Activity 3

Students compare two investments with different interest rates. Suggest to students that they look at the tables, changing the x-increase on the table when appropriate.

Answers to Calculator Activity

1. b. 12% for Lily's investments; 6% for Cameron's

   c. No. One investment's doubling time is 6.1 years and the other is 11.9.

   d. After 12.6 years

   e. After 25.2 years

2. c. No, although it is close. One investment's doubling time is 17.7 years and the other is 9 years.

   d. After 18.4 years

   e. After 36.7 years

3. c. No. One is 14.2 years and the other is 7.3 years.

   d. After 14.9 years

   e. After 29.8 years

Lesson 4

Semi-annual Investment Rates

Olivia invested $500 at 6% compounded semi-annually. This means 3% of the amount in the account is added to the account every 6 months.

1. Complete the table below showing Olivia's investment over time for 3.5 years.

Time (years)	Amount (dollars)
0	500
0.5	
1	
1.5	

2. The equation $y = 500(1 + 0.03)^{2x}$ can also be used to find the amount Olivia has in her account. Here x is the number of years and y is the amount.

   a. Check to see that each entry satisfies the equation $y = 500(1 + 0.03)^{2x}$.

   b. Use the equation $y = 500(1 + 0.03)^{2x}$ to find the amount invested after 5, 10, 20, and 30 years.

3. Graph the points in the table above. Draw a smooth curve to connect the points.

4. What does the y-intercept represent? Does the curve rise more and more steeply or more and more gently as time goes by?

5. What would an increase in the y-intercept mean? What would it mean if the curve rose more steeply earlier on?

A Visual Approach to Functions / © 2002 Key Curriculum Press

TEACHER NOTES

Students continue to study exponential growth in terms of money invested. In this lesson they are introduced to interest that is compounded semi-annually.

In Question 2, students take a leap and use the equation $y = 500(1 + 0.03)^{2x}$, where x is the number of years and y is the amount. Before they answer the second question, explain where that equation came from by working with them to develop the last column in the table below. A_0 is the starting amount.

Time (years)	Amount (dollars)	
0	500	A_0
0.5	515	$A_0(1 + .03)$
1	530.45	$A_0(1 + .03)(1 + .03) = A_0(1 + .03)^2$
1.5	546.36	$A_0(1 + .03)^2(1 + .03) = A_0(1 + .03)^3$
2	562.75	$A_0(1 + .03)^3(1 + .03) = A_0(1 + .03)^4$
2.5	579.64	$A_0(1 + .03)^4(1 + .03) = A_0(1 + .03)^5$
3	597.03	$A_0(1 + .03)^5(1 + .03) = A_0(1 + .03)^6$
3.5	614.94	$A_0(1 + .03)^6(1 + .03) = A_0(1 + .03)^7$

Answers

1. The table is shown above.

2. **a.** Each entry does satisfy the equation $y = 500(1 + 0.03)^{2x}$, where x is the number of years.

   b.

Time (years)	Amount (dollars)	
5	671.96	$A_0(1 + .03)^{10}$
10	903.06	$A_0(1 + .03)^{20}$
20	1,631	$A_0(1 + .03)^{40}$
30	2,945.8	$A_0(1 + .03)^{60}$

3.

4. The y-intercept represents the initial amount invested. The curve rises more steeply as time goes by.

5. An increase in the *y*-intercept would mean a bigger initial investment. If the curve rose more steeply earlier on, it would mean that the interest rate was higher.

Extension: See Calculator Activity 4

Students use the tangent function to find the slopes of two graphs. When they finish answering the first question, they may find it helpful to discuss that the slope of the line tangent to the curve is the slope of the curve at that point.

Answers to Calculator Activity

1. Both are increasing. $y = x$ increases at a constant rate, whereas $y = 1.03^{2x}$ increases at a steeper and steeper rate.

2. 1

3. When *x* increases from 47 to 48, *y* increases from 16.09 to 17.07. Before this point the change in *y* is less than 1, and after it the change is greater than 1.

4. The line looks parallel to $y = x$.

Lesson 5

Quarterly Investment Rates

Juan invested $1,000 in a bank account with 8% interest compounded quarterly.

1. Write an equation for the amount in Juan's account after every 3 months. Let NA = the new amount and A = the previous amount before interest is added.

2. The table below shows the amount in Juan's bank account over time. Complete the last two columns of the table.

Time (years)	Amount (dollars)	
0	1,000	A_0
0.25		$A_0(1 + .02)$
0.5		$A_0(1 + .02)(1 + .02) = A_0(1 + .02)^2$
0.75		
1		
1.25		
1.50		
1.75		

3. Check to see that each entry in the table above satisfies the equation $y = 1,000(1 + 0.02)^{4x}$, where x is the number of years and y is the amount.

4. Use the equation $y = 1,000(1 + 0.02)^{4x}$ to find the amount invested after 5, 10, 20, and 30 years.

5. Graph the points in the table above. Draw a smooth curve to connect the points.

6. What does the y-intercept represent? Does the curve rise more and more steeply or more and more gently as time goes by?

7. What would an increase in the y-intercept mean? What would it mean if the curve rose more steeply earlier on?

TEACHER NOTES

The focus of this lesson is determining the amount in an account with interest accruing every 3 months. Here, students develop the equation $y = 1{,}000(1 + 0.02)^{4x}$ (8% quarterly), where x is the number of years, y is the amount, and $1,000 is the initial investment.

Answers

1. $NA = A + 0.02A = (1 + 0.02)A$

2.

Time (years)	Amount (dollars)	
0	1,000	A_0
0.25	1,020	$A_0(1 + .02)$
0.5	1,040.40	$A_0(1 + .02)(1 + .02) = A_0(1 + .02)^2$
0.75	1,061.21	$A_0(1 + .02)^2 (1 + .02) = A_0(1 + .02)^3$
1	1,082.43	$A_0(1 + .02)^3 (1 + .02) = A_0(1 + .02)^4$
1.25	1,104.08	$A_0(1 + .02)^4 (1 + .02) = A_0(1 + .02)^5$
1.5	1,126.16	$A_0(1 + .02)^5 (1 + .02) = A_0(1 + .02)^6$
1.75	1,148.69	$A_0(1 + .02)^6 (1 + .02) = A_0(1 + .02)^7$

3. Each entry does satisfy the equation $y = 1{,}000(1 + 0.02)^{4x}$.

4.

Time (years)	Amount (dollars)	
5	1,485.95	$A_0(1 + .02)^{20}$
10	2,208.04	$A_0(1 + .02)^{40}$
20	4,875.44	$A_0(1 + .02)^{80}$
30	10,765.16	$A_0(1 + .02)^{120}$

5.

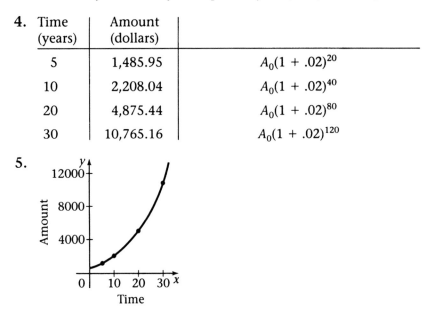

6. The y-intercept represents the initial amount Juan invested. The curve rises more steeply as time goes by.

7. An increase in the y-intercept would mean a bigger initial investment. If the curve rose more steeply earlier on, it would mean that the interest rate was higher.

Extension: See Calculator Activity 5 _____

Students repeat the activity from Calculator Activity 4 using $y = x$ and $y = 1.02^{4x}$.

Answers to Calculator Activity

1. Both are increasing. $y = x$ increases at a constant rate, whereas $y = 1.02^{4x}$ increases at a steeper and steeper rate.

2. 1

3. When x increases from 31 to 32, y increases from 11.653 to 12.613. Before this point the change in y is less than 1; the change is greater than 1 thereafter.

4. The line looks parallel to $y = x$.

Lesson 6

Filling In the Blanks

In Lessons 4 and 5, you saw examples of compounded interest. Fill in the blanks below to make up your own problem.

_____ invested $_____ at ___% compounded semi-annually. This means ___% of the amount in the account is added to the account _____. This can be represented symbolically by $NA = A + \_\_ \cdot A = (1 + \_\_)A$. Here NA stands for the new amount and A for the amount in the account just before interest is added.

1. Fill in the table below showing the investment over time.

Time (years)	Amount (dollars)	
0		A_0
		$A_0(1 + \_\_)$
		$A_0(1 + \_\_)(1 + \_\_) = A_0(1 + \_\_)^2$

2. Check to see that each entry satisfies the equation $y = \_\_(1 + \_\_)^{-x}$.

3. Use your equation from Question 2 to find the amount invested after 5, 10, 20, and 30 years.

4. Graph the points. Draw a smooth curve to connect the points.

5. What does the y-intercept represent? Does the curve rise more and more steeply or more and more gently as time goes by?

6. What would an increase in the y-intercept mean? What would it mean if the curve rose more steeply earlier on?

TEACHER NOTES

Students create their own investment scenario to investigate exponential growth.

This lesson should be given only if students have a good sense of the pattern developed in the previous two lessons. You may want to have them work in pairs with two pairs helping each other with their different choices.

Answers

1. The dollar amount is A_0. The half of the percentage rate goes in the blanks provided in the table, because interest is compounded semi-annually.

2. Let the percentage rate be r and the initial amount be A_0. The equation is $y = A_0(1 + 0.5r)^{2x}$.

3–6. Answers will vary.

Lesson 7

Investment Equations

When a person invests P dollars at r% where the interest is compounded n times a year, the amount in the account after t years is given by the equation $P\left(1 + 0.01\frac{r}{n}\right)^{nt}$.

1. Gina invests $890 at 7% compounded quarterly. Choose the equation that gives the amount of Gina's investment over time in years.

   A. $y = 890(1 + 0.07)^{4t}$

   B. $y = 890(1 + 0.0175)^{4t}$

   C. $y = 890(1 + 0.07)^{t}$

2. For each of the equations you did not choose in Question 1, write a sentence that corresponds to it.

3. Sam invests $8,850 at 12% compounded monthly. Choose the equation that gives the amount of Sam's investment over time in years.

   A. $y = 8,850(1 + 0.01)^{12t}$

   B. $y = 8,850(1 + 0.12)^{t}$

   C. $y = 8,850(1 + 0.012)^{12t}$

4. For each of the equations you did not choose in Question 3, write a sentence that corresponds to it.

5. Desi invests $4,500 at 10% compounded daily. Write the equation that gives the amount of Desi's investment over time in years.

6. Raul invests $2,500 at 6.5% compounded hourly. Write the equation that gives the amount of Raul's investment over time in years.

TEACHER NOTES

The focus of this lesson is to get students to find the amount of an investment where interest is compounded at times other than annually, semi-annually, and quarterly using the equation $P\left(1 + 0.01\frac{r}{n}\right)^{nt}$. Here P is the initial investment in dollars at $r\%$ where the interest is compounded n times a year.

Answers

1. Equation B

2. Equation A. $y = 890(1 + 0.07)^{4t}$ would model a situation in which $890 was invested at 28% compounded quarterly. Finding such an investment would be another matter.

   Equation C. $y = 890(1 + 0.07)^{t}$ would model a situation in which $890 was invested at 7% compounded annually.

3. Equation A

4. Equation B. $y = 8{,}850(1 + 0.12)^{t}$ would model a situation in which $8,850 was invested at 12% compounded annually.

   Equation C. $y = 8{,}850(1 + 0.012)^{12t}$ would model a situation in which $8,850 was invested at 14.4% compounded monthly.

5. $y = 4{,}500(1 + 0.00027)^{365x}$ where y is the amount after x years.

6. $y = 2{,}500(1 + 0.0000074)^{8760x}$ where y is the amount after x years.

Extension: See Calculator Activity 7 _____

Students investigate the effects of different compounding intervals (annual, semi-annual, quarterly, monthly, daily, and hourly) on an investment.

Answers to Calculator Activity

2. $0.18

3. $3.13

4. $184

5. $3,127

Lesson 8

Comparing Population and Investment

You may remember from previous lessons that investments and populations have similar functions.

Suppose the population of Jay's hometown is decreasing by 4% each year. You can picture this by thinking that each year 4% of the population leaves and no one takes their place. You can write this as the function $NP = P - 0.04P = (1 - 0.04)P$. Here NP stands for the new population and P for the population the year before.

1. The table below shows the population of Jay's hometown over time. Complete the table. Assume the initial population is 50,000.

Time (years)	Population	
0	50,000	P_0
1		$P_0(1 - .04)$
2		$P_0(1 - .04)(1 - .04) = P_0(1 - .04)^2$
3		

2. Check to see that each entry satisfies the equation $y = 50{,}000(1 - 0.04)^x$.

3. Use the equation $y = 50{,}000(1 - 0.04)^x$ to find the number of people in the city after 10, 20, and 40 years.

4. Graph the points in the table. Be sure to draw a smooth curve to connect the points.

5. What does the y-intercept represent? Does the curve fall more steeply or more gently as time goes by?

6. What would an increase in the y-intercept mean? What would it mean if the curve fell more steeply earlier on?

7. What is the difference between an exponential growth equation and an exponential decay (or decrease) equation?

In the previous lessons, students looked at many exponential functions for investments where an initial amount grows at a certain percentage rate. Here, they look at an exponential function where the initial amount decreases by a certain percentage each year.

    Students answer questions similar to those they encountered before. They may benefit from a discussion of other examples demonstrating the same concept explored in this lesson.

Answers

1.

Time (years)	Population	
0	50,000	P_0
1	48,000	$P_0(1 - .04)$
2	46,080	$P_0(1 - .04)(1 - .04) = P_0(1 - .04)^2$
3	44,237	$P_0(1 - .04)^2(1 - .04) = P_0(1 - .04)^3$
4	42,467	$P_0(1 - .04)^3(1 - .04) = P_0(1 - .04)^4$
5	40,769	$P_0(1 - .04)^4(1 - .04) = P_0(1 - .04)^5$
6	39,138	$P_0(1 - .04)^5(1 - .04) = P_0(1 - .04)^6$
7	37,572	$P_0(1 - .04)^6(1 - .04) = P_0(1 - .04)^7$

2. Each entry does satisfy the equation $y = 50,000(1 - 0.04)^x$.

3. The population after 10, 20, and 40 years is 33,242; 22,100; and 9,768 respectively.

4.

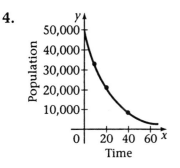

5. The y-intercept represents the initial population. The curve falls more gently.

6. An increase in the y-intercept would mean more people in the town initially. If the curve fell more steeply earlier on, it would mean people were leaving at a higher percentage rate each year.

7. Using the general form $y = ab^x$, the growth equation has a b-value greater than 1. The decay equation has a b-value less than 1.

Lesson 9

Summarizing Exponential Functions

1. Consider the following chart comparing exponential functions. The first line has been done for you. Complete the table.

Function	Initial Value	Growth or Decline?	Percentage of Change	Sketch a Graph
$7,500(1 + .03)^t$	7,500	growth	3%	
$80,000(1 - .07)^t$				
$90,000(1 + .02)^t$				
$52,000(1 - .065)^t$				

2. For each of the functions in the table, write a sentence that matches the function.

3. Write a paragraph summarizing what you know about functions of the type $y = ab^x$. In your summary, describe what happens when b is greater than 1 and when b is less than 1 but more than 0.

 A Visual Approach to Functions / © 2002 Key Curriculum Press

This lesson can be used as a review or quiz.

Answers

1.

Function	Initial Value	Growth or Decline?	Percentage of Change	Sketch a Graph
$7{,}500(1 + .03)^t$	7,500	growth	3%	*(graph: increasing curve, Value vs. Time)*
$80{,}000(1 - .07)^t$	80,000	decline	7%	*(graph: decreasing curve, Value vs. Time)*
$90{,}000(1 + .02)^t$	90,000	growth	2%	*(graph: increasing curve, Value vs. Time)*
$52{,}000(1 - .065)^t$	52,000	decline	6.5%	*(graph: decreasing curve, Value vs. Time)*

2. Sample sentences:

   Jason's initial investment of $7,500 has increased by 3% each year.

   The initial population 80,000 fell each year by 7% as people moved to the city.

   Ginger invested $90,000, and it increased by 2% each year.

   The $52,000 car decreased in value by 6.5% each year.

3. Functions of the type $y = ab^x$ are called exponential functions, where a and b are constants. When b is between 0 and 1, the function decreases. When b is greater than 1, the function increases.

Chapter 4 | Calculator Activities

Calculator Activity 1: Investment Equations

1. **a.** Enter $Y_1 = 50\left(2^{x/7}\right)$ into your calculator. Graph the equation using a window where x varies from 0 to 47 and y from 0 to 300.

    b. How can you find the doubling time for this exponential function using only the ⟦TRACE⟧ key?

    c. If the function describes growth of an investment over time in years, what will the investment be worth after 14 years? When will it be at $200?

    d. Look at the investment after 1 year. When will that amount double?

2. Repeat Question 1 for $Y_1 = 60\left(2^{x/8}\right)$.

3. Repeat Question 1 for $Y_1 = 50\left(2^{x/12}\right)$.

4. Compare the three functions.

Calculator Activity 2: Compounding Interest

Three friends put money into separate bank accounts. Each account compounds the interest annually. Sara invested $100 at an 8% interest rate. Hannah invested $100 at a 6% interest rate. Jerome invested the same amount at a 10% interest rate.

1. Enter $Y_1 = 100(1 + 0.08)^x$ for Sara's investment over time. Enter $Y_2 = 100(1 + 0.06)^x$ for Hannah's investment and $Y_3 = 100(1 + 0.10)^x$ for Jerome's investment.

2. To compare the doubling times for the three curves, graph the line $Y_4 = 200$ and look at its intersection with each of the curves. Write as many observations as you can about the doubling time for the three investments.

3. Based on those graphs, predict what the doubling time is for investments at interest rates of 4% and 12%.

4. Is the doubling time for 8% twice that as for 4%?

   A Visual Approach to Functions / © 2002 Key Curriculum Press

1. Lily and Cameron each invested $100. Cameron's account yields 6% interest compounded annually. Lily's account gives 12% interest compounded annually. The equations $Y_1 = 100(1.06)^x$ and $Y_2 = 100(1.12)^x$ represent their two investments.

   a. Enter both equations into your calculator.

   b. Look at both tables. What is the annual rate for each account?

   c. Is the doubling time for Cameron's investment twice that for Lily's investment? What are their doubling times?

   d. When will Lily's investment be twice Cameron's investment?

   e. When will Lily's investment be four times Cameron's investment?

Repeat the exercise for the following investments. What observations can you make?

2. 4% and 8% interest

3. 5% and 10% interest

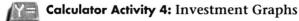

 Calculator Activity 4: Investment Graphs

Graph $y = x$ and $y = 1.03^{2x}$ and find a good viewing window for the graphs.

1. Describe both functions.

2. What is the slope of $y = x$?

3. In the second function, when x changes by 1, where is the change in y close to 1?

4. Use Tangent (under the Draw menu) to draw a line tangent to the curve at the point where the change in y is close to 1. What do you notice?

Calculator Activity 5: More Investment Graphs

Graph $y = x$ and $y = 1.02^{4x}$ on an interval from 0 to 94 for both x and y.

1. Describe both functions.

2. What is the slope of $y = x$?

3. In the second function, when x changes by 1, where is the change in y close to 1?

4. Use the Tangent function to draw a line tangent to the curve at that point. What do you notice?

Calculator Activity 7: Comparing Investments

1. Enter six equations for a $100 investment corresponding to six different types of compounding interest (annual, semi-annual, quarterly, monthly, daily, and hourly). Use an interest rate of 6%.

2. After 1 year, what is the difference between the amount accumulated for the investment where compounding was annual and the amount where compounding was hourly?

3. If the money was left in the account for 10 years, what would the difference be?

4. If the initial investment was $100,000, what would the difference be after 1 year?

5. If this money was left in the account for 10 years, what would the difference be?

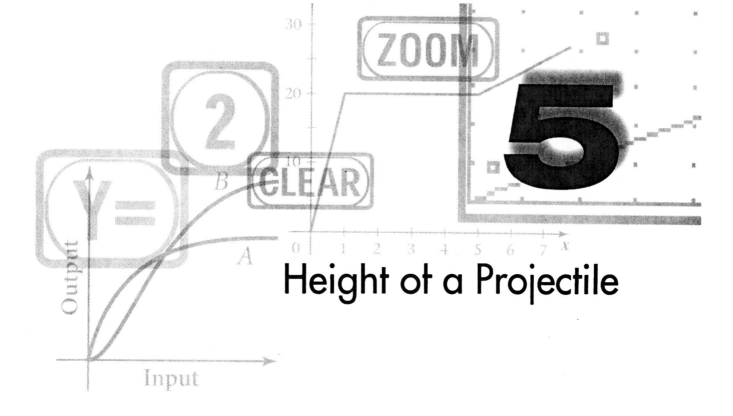

Height of a Projectile

This chapter introduces students to quadratic functions. Students take a look at quadratic functions by considering the relationship between the height of a projectile and time elapsed since firing. As in previous lessons, they first look at qualitative graphs and then move on to quantitative graphs and tables. Students investigate the basic shape of the graphs using what the shape tells them about the motion of a projectile. They then explore equations that represent the paths of projectiles over time.

Lesson 1

Projectile Motion

Choose the graph that shows each projectile's height as time goes on.

1. Lydia fired a model rocket vertically upward into the air.

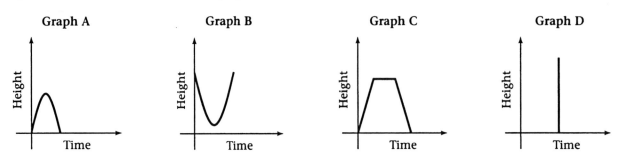

2. While standing on top of a building, Alexander threw a ball vertically upward into the air.

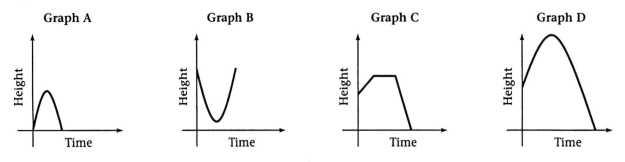

3. Nathaniel shot his model rocket from the ground into the air. It landed on top of a building.

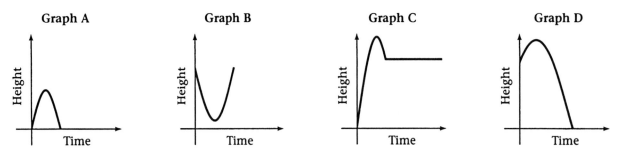

4. Lonnie fired a model rocket. It was a dud and did not lift off the ground.

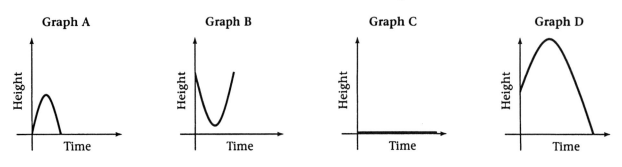

A Visual Approach to Functions / © 2002 Key Curriculum Press

TEACHER NOTES

Students are introduced to quadratic functions by considering the relationship between the height of a projectile and the time elapsed since firing. In this lesson, they study qualitative graphs to familiarize themselves with the overall shape of a parabola.

In Question 1, students often choose Graph D. You may want to emphasize that with a function, each element in the domain corresponds to one and only one element in the range. Specifically, for each moment in time there corresponds one and only one height.

Students may benefit from a closer look at the graphs. For Question 3, you can ask students what a horizontal line corresponds to in terms of this example. (A period of time when the height above the ground does not change.)

Answers

1. Graph A
2. Graph D
3. Graph C
4. Graph C

Extension: See Calculator Activity 1

Students investigate parabolic functions. They explore which equations increase, then decrease, and vice versa.

Answers to Calculator Activity

3. Negative values of A make the graph increase, and then decrease. Positive values of A make the graph decrease, and then increase.

Lesson 2
Height and Time Relationships

Sonya and Laura were having a contest to see who could throw a ball higher into the air. Each graph shows the relationship between the height and time elapsed for the two balls. The shape of this graph is called a parabola.

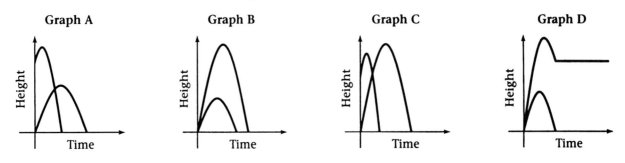

1. For each graph, describe the height as a function of time for the two balls. Include as many observations and comparisons as you can.

   Graph A:

   Graph B:

   Graph C:

   Graph D:

2. Do any of the graphs represent a situation where one ball went higher than the other but spent less time in the air? Is this possible? Explain.

3. Is it possible that the balls were several hundred feet away from each other when they were thrown upward?

4. Is it possible that a ball came back down to the spot where it was thrown?

A Visual Approach to Functions / © 2002 Key Curriculum Press

TEACHER NOTES

For Question 2, you may want to point out to students that in order to decide which ball stays in the air longer in Graphs A, B, and C, they need only look at the *x*-intercepts. In Graph D, they must decide if the *x*-intercept comes before or after the spot where the piecewise function changes from the first branch to the second.

For Questions 3 and 4, you may want to restate that the *x*-axis represents time traveled since throwing, not horizontal distance.

Answers

1. Graph A: One ball is thrown from above the ground. It goes higher but lands before the second ball, which is thrown from the ground.

    Graph B: Both balls are thrown from the ground. One goes higher and stays in the air longer than the other.

    Graph C: One ball is thrown from above the ground and the other is thrown from the ground. The second ball goes higher and stays in the air longer.

    Graph D: Both balls are thrown from the ground. The one that goes higher lands above the ground, at the same time the other ball lands on the ground.

2. Yes, Graph A represents this situation because one ball was thrown from a much higher spot.

3. Yes, the function only describes height above the ground over time. Horizontal distance of the balls is not taken into account.

4. Yes, because there is no information about the horizontal distance.

Extension: See Calculator Activity 2 _____

Students explore maximum and minimum values for a parabolic function.

Answers to Calculator Activities

1. At $x = 2$, the function achieves a maximum value of $y = 4$.
2. You would use a curve that increases, and then decreases.
3. You would use a curve that decreases, and then increases.

Lesson 3

Interpreting Key Points

1. Simone shot a flare vertically into the air. The graph shows the flare's height above the ground over time elapsed since firing. Decide which sentence is a good match for the graph.

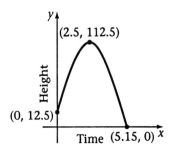

A. Simone fired the flare from the ground. It reached its maximum height of 112.5 feet after 2.5 seconds.

B. The flare was fired from a platform 5.15 feet above the ground and reached a maximum height of 112.5 feet after 2.5 seconds.

C. The flare was fired from a platform 12.5 feet above the ground, reached a maximum height of 112.5 feet, and stayed in the air for 5.15 seconds.

D. Simone's flare reached a height of 100 feet after 2.5 seconds.

2. How long did Simone's flare stay in the air? How high above the ground did the flare go? How long did it take for the flare to reach this height? How many feet did Simone's flare rise? How many feet did it fall?

3. For each sentence you did not choose in Question 1, draw a graph that could correspond to it.

TEACHER NOTES

The objective of this lesson is for students to get a feel for the meaning of the vertex, *y*-intercept, and *x*-intercept of a quadratic function modeling height of a projectile over time. Here students look at graphs of quadratic functions with key points indicated.

You may want to discuss with students that the graph of a quadratic function is a parabola. Also discuss when the parabola is curved upward and when downward.

For Question 3, Graph D, point out that because the maximum height is not mentioned, the flare may reach past 100 feet. Therefore, the graph does not have to show 100 feet as the maximum height. The maximum height the flare reached should be no less than 100 feet.

Answers

1. Sentence C

2. Simone's flare stayed in the air for 5.15 seconds. It reached a height of 112.5 feet. It took 2.5 seconds. The flare rose for 100 feet and fell for 112.5 feet.

3.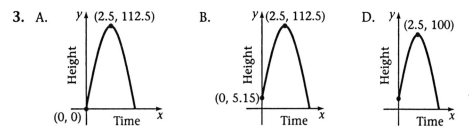

 Extension: See Calculator Activity 3 _____

In this lesson, students practice interpreting points in terms of height and time.

Lesson 4

Graphs from Key Points

Andrea and Juan fired their model rockets straight up into the air several times. The graphs show the heights of their rockets as time passed.

1. Andrea fired her rocket from a platform 7 feet above the ground. Her rocket reached its maximum height of 232 feet after 3.75 seconds and was in the air for 7.6 seconds. Choose the graph that best matches the description of Andrea's rocket.

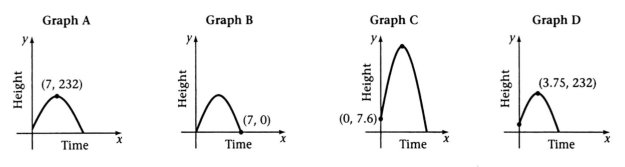

2. For each graph you did not choose in Question 1, write a sentence that describes the information given.

3. Juan fired his rocket from a platform 2 meters above the ground. It reached a maximum height of 136 meters after 2.86 seconds and stayed in the air for 5.78 seconds. Choose the graph that best matches the description of Juan's rocket.

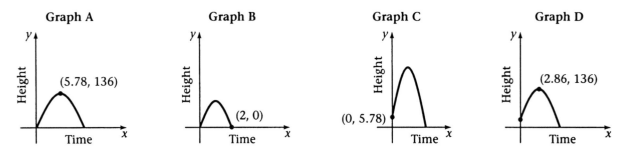

4. For each graph you did not choose in Question 3, write a sentence that describes the information given.

TEACHER NOTES

As in the previous lesson, students look at graphs of quadratic functions with key points indicated. They continue to investigate the vertex, *y*-intercept, and *x*-intercept of a graph modeling height of a projectile over time. Students should also be getting the idea that when an object is thrown or fired vertically upward, the shape of the graph is a parabola. The initial height or max height may change, but the shape of the parabola does not change.

The first set of graphs gives the height of the rocket in feet; the second set gives the height in meters.

Answers

1. Graph D

2. Graph A: After 7 seconds, the rocket was 232 feet in the air.

    Graph B: The rocket was in the air for 7 seconds.

    Graph C: Andrea's rocket was fired from a platform 7.6 feet above the ground.

3. Graph D

4. Graph A: After 5.78 seconds the rocket was, at its highest point, 136 feet in the air.

    Graph B: The rocket was in the air for 2 seconds.

    Graph C: Juan's rocket was fired from a platform 5.78 meters above the ground.

Lesson 5

Describing and Drawing

1. The graphs below represent the flight of Josh's flare. Height is measured in feet, and time is measured in seconds. For each graph, describe the motion. Give as many details as you can.

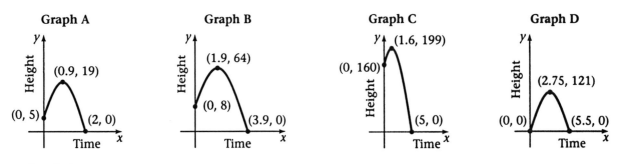

Graph A   Graph B   Graph C   Graph D

a. Graph A:

b. Graph B:

c. Graph C:

d. Graph D:

2. The sentences below describe the relationship between height of a projectile and time. Draw a graph that could match each description.

   a. A projectile was fired into the air from a platform 10 feet above the ground. After 3.3 seconds it reached its maximum height of 192 feet. It hit the ground after 6.8 seconds.

   b. Laura fired her model rocket into the air from the ground. After 1.8 seconds it reached its maximum height of 52.6 feet. Her rocket hit the ground after 3.6 seconds.

A Visual Approach to Functions / © 2002 Key Curriculum Press

TEACHER NOTES

In this lesson, students continue to look at quadratic functions modeled as the height of projectiles over time. Students move further in this lesson, as they must draw graphs as well as interpret them.

By the end of this lesson, students should have a good grasp of the y-intercept, the x-intercepts, and the vertex of a quadratic function. You will want to discuss these key points, because they describe the path of a projectile.

You may also want to discuss what happens when meters are used instead of feet as the measure of height. Discuss what happens to the graph. This will be helpful in preparation for Lesson 6.

Answers

1. a. Graph A: The flare is thrown upward from a platform 5 feet above the ground, reaches a maximum height of 19 feet after 0.9 second, and stays in the air for a total of 2 seconds.

    b. Graph B: The flare is fired from a platform 8 feet above the ground, reaches a maximum height of 64 feet after 1.9 seconds, and stays in the air for a total of 3.9 seconds.

    c. Graph C: The flare is thrown upward from a platform 160 feet above the ground, reaches a maximum height of 199 feet after 1.6 seconds, and stays in the air for a total of 5 seconds.

    d. Graph D: The flare is fired from the ground, reaches a maximum height of 121 feet after 2.75 seconds, and stays in the air for a total of 5.5 seconds.

2. a.   b.

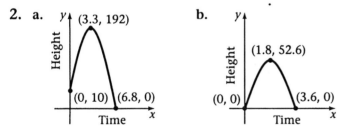

▣ Extension: See Calculator Activity 5 _____

Students practice interpreting x-intercepts and the vertex.

Answers to Calculator Activity

2. The vertex is at the point (2.34, 91.89), and the *x*-intercepts are at (−0.05, 0) and (4.74, 0).

3. The rocket reaches a maximum height of 91.89 feet at time 2.34 seconds.

4. The graph looks almost horizontal near the vertex.

5. The *y*-values will be closer together at each interval.

6. After 4.74 seconds the rocket lands on the ground.

7. The graph looks very steep close to the *x*-intercept.

8. The *y*-values will be farther apart at each interval.

Lesson 6

Using Initial Velocity

Suppose a rocket is fired upward from the ground. The height of the rocket as a function of time can be written using function notation as $h(t)$. The height at the beginning can be written as $h(0)$ or h_0.

The height (in feet) of the rocket above the ground is given by $h(t) = -16t^2 + v_0t + h_0$ where h_0 is its initial height, v_0 is its initial velocity, and -16 represents gravity pulling down on it. If the rocket is fired from the ground, $h_0 = 0$.

1. Suppose Lynda fires a model rocket from the ground with an initial velocity of 72 feet per second.

   a. What is the equation for the height, $h(t)$, of the rocket? Explain why this is equivalent to $h(t) = -8t(2t - 9)$.

   b. For what values of t does $h(t)$ equal 0? What do these values tell you about the rocket?

   c. Plot those points on the graph at right.

   d. Explain the significance of the point midway between these two points.

   e. What is the maximum height of the rocket? Plot that point on the graph.

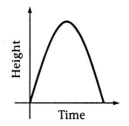

2. Suppose a rocket is fired from the ground with an initial velocity of 96 feet per second.

   a. What is the equation for the height, $h(t)$, of the rocket?

   b. What is the maximum height the rocket reaches?

   c. How long will the rocket be in the air?

   d. Draw the graph of the motion and put in the important points.

3. Suppose a rocket is fired from the ground with an initial velocity of 21 meters per second. When we use meters instead of feet, the -16 changes to -4.9 and the equation becomes $h(t) = -4.9t^2 + v_0t + h_0$.

   a. What is the equation for the height, $h(t)$, of this rocket? Explain why this equation is equivalent to $h(t) = -0.7t(7t - 30)$.

   b. For what values of t does $h(t)$ equal 0? What do these values tell you about the rocket?

   c. Plot these points on the graph at right.

   d. Explain the significance of the point midway between these two points.

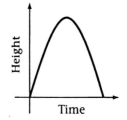

TEACHER NOTES

In this lesson, students explore parabolas of the form $y = bx(x - a)$ that model rockets fired from the ground. They take a big leap here when they look at the algebraic equations. They are also introduced to function notation, $h(t)$, for height as a function of time.

Remind students that, normally, distance equals speed multiplied by time, as in the speed of a car on a highway in Chapter 1. However, when an object is thrown upward, it also has gravity pulling it down, so the equation for the height becomes $h(t) = v_0 t - 16t^2 + h_0$. In this equation, h_0 is the initial height above the ground, if the object did not start out at ground level. The coefficient, 16, comes from the Earth's gravity. (On another planet, or on the moon, the coefficient is a different number. Or if we were using metric measurements, the coefficient would be 4.9)

You may want to discuss factoring before they begin the lesson. Mention that they can also expand equations to make sure they are the same. Students will benefit from an explanation of the vertex, y-intercept, and x-intercept (if any) in terms of the quadratic function.

Answers

1. **a.** The equation is $h(t) = -16t^2 + 72t$. Factoring out $-8t$, you get
    $h(t) = -8t(2t - 9)$.

    b. Each choice of 0 and $\frac{9}{2}$ for t makes $h(t)$ equal 0. This indicates that the rocket is fired from the ground and hits the ground after $\frac{9}{2}$ seconds. (The points are the x-intercepts for the parabola.)

    c. See graph below.

    d. The point midway between the two gives the x-coordinate of the vertex $\left(\frac{9}{4}\right)$, where the rocket is at its maximum height.

    e. The maximum height is 81 feet.

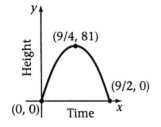

A Visual Approach to Functions

2. **a.** The equation is $h(t) = -16t^2 + 96t$. This is equivalent to
$h(t) = -16t(t - 6)$.

   b. The rocket reaches its maximum height of 144 feet (after 3 seconds).

   c. The rocket will be in the air for 6 seconds.

   d.

3. **a.** The equation is $h(t) = -4.9t^2 + 21t$. Factoring out $-0.7t$ leads to the
representation $h(t) = -0.7t(7t - 30)$.

   b. Each choice of 0 and $\frac{30}{7}$ for t makes $h(t)$ equal 0. The first indicates that
the rocket is fired from the ground, and the second indicates that the
rocket hits the ground after $\frac{30}{7}$ seconds. The points are the x-intercepts
for the parabola.

   c.

   d. The point midway between the two points gives the x-coordinate $\left(\frac{15}{7}\right)$,
where the rocket is at its maximum height.

▶ Extension: See Calculator Activity 6 _____

Students explore table values and discover the symmetric nature of
parabolas. The activity also shows how different forms of an equation
reveal very different aspects of a function.

Answers to Calculator Activity

1. **b.** The Y_1 values increase then decrease. The increments in Y_1 are first
5, then 3, then 1. After this, Y_1 decreases in the same manner, first
by 1, then by 3, then by 5.

   c. The value of Y_1 is 65 at both 1.25 and 3.25. The pattern continues.

   d. The values for Y_1 and Y_2 are identical.

   e. Multiply both out.

Lesson 7
Equivalent Equations

Recall the equation used for finding the height (in feet) of a rocket from Lesson 6. These three equations are all equivalent, but factored differently.

A. $h(t) = -16t^2 + 160t + 176$

B. $h(t) = -16(t - 5)^2 + 576$

C. $h(t) = -16(t + 1)(t - 11)$

1. Expand Equations B and C. Compare them to Equation A.

2. What is the initial height of the rocket above the ground? Which one of the three equivalent forms shows the initial height? Where does it appear?

3. How long will it take the rocket to hit the ground? Which one of the three equivalent forms shows this time? Explain.

4. How long does it take the rocket to reach its maximum height? What is the maximum height the rocket reaches? Which one of the three equivalent forms shows these values?

5. What is the initial velocity of the rocket? Which one of the three equivalent forms shows this value? Explain.

6. Sketch the graph of the rocket, putting in the appropriate points.

The objective of this lesson is to get students to recognize and compare equivalent equations for a parabola. Students need to remember that equivalent equations all represent the same set of points. Each form of the equation, however, highlights different information about the situation.

For any function modeling the height of a projectile over time, there are three important equivalent forms of the equation:

$$y = ax^2 + bx + c$$

This reveals the initial height and initial velocity.

$$y = a\left(x + \frac{b}{2a}\right)^2 + c - \left(\frac{b^2}{4a}\right)$$

This reveals the vertex, which gives the maximum height and time it takes to reach this maximum height.

$$y = a\left(x + \frac{b + \sqrt{b^2 - (4ac)}}{2a}\right)\left(x + \frac{b - \sqrt{b^2 - (4ac)}}{2a}\right)$$

This reveals the x-intercepts. The larger of the two intercepts corresponds to the time the projectile is in the air. For the general case, x-intercepts occur if and only if $b^2 - 4ac \geq 0$.

Students might not recognize the equivalence of the three algebraic representations of the situation. Before they expand equations in Question 1, you might ask them how they can tell that each of the equations represents a parabola.

Answers

2. The initial height is 176 feet, which equation A reveals. The original height appears as a constant at the end of the equation.

3. It will take 11 seconds to hit the ground. Equation C reveals this value. You need to let $h(t)$ equal 0 and then solve for t.

4. It takes 5 seconds to reach the maximum height of 576 feet. Equation B reveals both of these values.

5. The initial velocity of the rocket is 160 feet per second. The first form shows the answer as long as you know the height of a projectile above the ground is modeled by $h(t) = -16t^2 + v_0 t + h_0$ where h_0 is the initial height and v_0 is the initial velocity.

6.

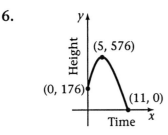

 Extension: See Calculator Activity 7 _____

Answers to Calculator Activity

1. **a.** The equation is $y = -16(x - 6)^2 + 600$.

    b. The x-values should go from 0 to 13 and the y-values from 0 to 650.

    c. The initial height is 24 feet and the time in the air is 12.1 seconds.

2. You can find the initial velocity by expanding the equation to get the coefficient of x as $14 \times 16 = 224$. Some students may see this pattern and arrive at the answer without expanding.

    a. The equation is $-16(x - 7)^2 + 800$.

    b. The x-values should go from 0 to 15 and the y-values from 0 to 850.

    c. The initial height is 16 feet and the time in the air is 14.1 seconds.

Lesson 8

Launching Fireworks

At the yearly fireworks display, a rocket is launched into the air with an initial speed of 95 feet per second, from a platform that is 8 feet above the ground.

1. What is the function $h(t)$ that models the path of the rocket? Let t represent the number of seconds elapsed since firing and $h(t)$ represent the height of the firecracker in feet.

   Use your graphing calculator to answer the following questions about the path of the rocket. Round your answers to two decimal places. Don't forget to include units.

2. **a.** How high is the rocket after $1\frac{1}{2}$ seconds?

   b. Use an algebraic method to find the answer to part a. What is the equation you used?

3. **a.** When is the rocket 100 feet above the ground? Is there more than one answer to this question? Explain your answer.

   b. Use an algebraic method to find the answer to part a. What is the equation you used?

4. How high does the rocket go? When does it reach this height?

5. When does the rocket land?

6. Sketch a graph of the function. Make sure to include appropriate scales along each axis.

7. Suppose the y-intercept is increased by 2. What does this tell you about the rocket?

TEACHER NOTES

The focus of this lesson is to bring together the ideas presented in Lessons 6 and 7. Students should do this lesson with the aid of a graphing calculator.

Writing the equation is challenging, but students feel a sense of accomplishment after finishing this problem.

Students will need to know the quadratic formula to solve the equation in Question 3b.

Answers

1. The function is $h(t) = -16t^2 + 95t + 8$.

2. **a.** After 1.5 seconds the rocket is 114.5 feet above the ground.

   b. You need to solve $h = -16\left(\frac{3}{2}\right)^2 + 95\left(\frac{3}{2}\right) + 8$. Solving this equation gives $h = 114.5$ as well.

3. **a.** At both 1.22 and 4.72 seconds, the rocket is 100 feet above the ground. There are two answers as it is 100 feet above the ground on the way up and on the way down. You can find these answers by looking at the table, intersecting the function with the line $y = 100$, or by using the quadratic formula.

   b. You need to solve $100 = -16t^2 + 95t + 8$ for t. You can do this by using the quadratic formula.

4. The rocket reaches a height of 149.02 feet at 2.97 seconds.

5. It lands after 6.02 seconds.

6.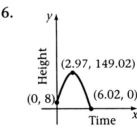

7. It is launched from 10 feet rather than 8 feet.

Extension: See Calculator Activity 8 _____

Answers to Calculator Activity

2. As K gets larger, the parabola shifts up and to the right.

3. An initial speed of 112 feet per second leads to a maximum height of 200 feet.

Lesson 9

Comparing Paths

1. If two identical rockets are fired straight up into the sky, even if they are fired 3 seconds apart, their paths are identical. Which graph shows this situation?

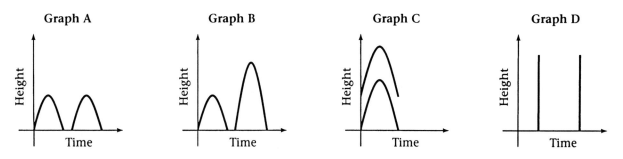

2. These graphs represent the height in feet of two rockets that are fired from the ground 9 seconds apart but have identical paths.

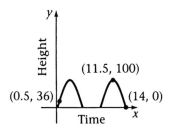

a. For each point indicated on one curve, find a corresponding point on the other curve. Label each new point with the correct coordinates.

b. How long is each rocket in the air?

c. How high does each rocket go?

d. How long does it take each rocket to reach its maximum height after blastoff?

e. Complete the table for the two rockets.

Time (seconds)	Height of First Rocket (feet)	Height of Second Rocket (feet)
0	0	0
1	64	0
2	96	0
3		
4		
5		
6		
7		
8		
9		
10		
11		
12	0	96
13	0	64
14	0	0

3. The height of the first rocket is given by the function $h(t) = -16t^2 + 80t$. We can find this equation using the vertex or the x-intercepts. The vertex gives $h(t) = -16(t - 2.5)^2 + 100$ and the x-intercept gives $h(t) = -16t(t - 5)$. Choose three different points from the table for the first rocket. Do they satisfy the function? What do you think the function is for the second rocket?

TEACHER NOTES

In this lesson, students look at two rockets that are fired at different times but have identical paths.

Given the function for the first rocket, Question 3 asks students to write the function that will give the height of the second rocket. Students may find it beneficial to have the following hint: To find the same heights for the second rocket as for the first rocket, choose values for t that are 9 larger.

Answers

1. Graph A

2. a.
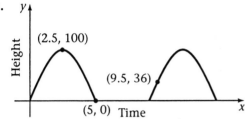

   b. The rockets are in the air for 5 seconds. (We know the first x-intercept on the second curve is (9, 0), so we see the rocket is in the air for 5 seconds.)

   c. They reach a height of 100 feet.

   d. It takes the rockets 2.5 seconds to reach their maximum heights.

   e.

Time (seconds)	Height of First Rocket (feet)	Height of Second Rocket (feet)
0	0	0
1	64	0
2	96	0
3	96	0
4	64	0
5	0	0
6	0	0
7	0	0
8	0	0
9	0	0
10	0	64
11	0	96
12	0	96
13	0	64
14	0	0

3. The points do satisfy the function. The second function is
$y = -16(t - 9)^2 + 80(t - 9)$.

⌨ Extension: See Calculator Activity 9 ⎯⎯⎯⎯⎯⎯⎯⎯⎯⎯⎯

Students generally don't have trouble with vertical translations, but horizontal translations do not come as naturally. Asking them "What do we need to do to get the same *y*-values?" is helpful.

Answers to Calculator Activity

2.

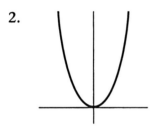

3. The *x*-values must be 3 larger than the former *x*-values to counteract the −3.

5. It will shift the curve 3 units to the right.

Lesson 10

Comparing Equations

1. Jason fired his model rocket from the ground at 95 feet per second. James fired his rocket at the same velocity 6 seconds later. What are the equations that model the heights of the rockets over time elapsed since the first rocket was fired? Fill them in the blanks for y_1 and y_2 below.

2. Graph both equations on the axes below, indicating how high each rocket goes and how long it is in the air.

3. Fill in the table below, putting in zeros where appropriate. You can stop at the point where the second rocket reaches the ground.

Graph

Algebraic Representations

$y_1 = $ _____

$y_2 = $ _____

Table

Time (seconds)	Height of First Rocket (feet)	Height of Second Rocket (feet)
0		
1		
2		
3		
4		
5		
6		
7		
8		
9		
10		
11		
12		
13		
14		

TEACHER NOTES

Students create the graph, table, and equation for two rockets fired at different times with the same initial velocity. As in Lesson 9, they determine the functions that describe both rockets and create a graph and table of the information.

Answers

1. The equations are $y = -16x^2 + 95x$ and $y = -16(x - 6)^2 + 95(x - 6)$ where y is height above the ground and x is seconds elapsed since the first rocket was fired.

2. The model predicts that the rockets go up approximately 141 feet in the air and are in the air for about 5.9 seconds.

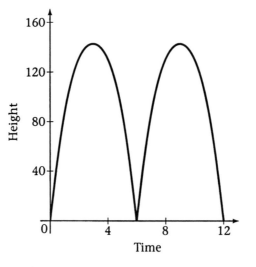

3.

Time (seconds)	Height of Jason's Rocket (feet)	Height of James's Rocket (feet)
0	0	0
1	79	0
2	126	0
3	141	0
4	124	0
5	75	0
6	0	0
7	0	79
8	0	126
9	0	141
10	0	124
11	0	75
12	0	0

Calculator Activity 1: Increasing and Decreasing Functions

1. Enter $Y_1 = A(x - B)^2 + C$ into the calculator.
   Enter -1 [STO] A:2 [STO] B:4 [STO] C into the Home screen.

2. Graph the equation using an interval for x from -10 to 10 and for y from -10 to 10. Notice that the function first increases and then decreases as you move from left to right.

3. Try different values for A, B, and C. Which values make the graph increase, and then decrease? Which values make the graph decrease, and then increase?

 Calculator Activity 2: Real World Increasing and Decreasing Functions

Repeat steps 1 and 2 from Calculator Activity 1 and answer the following questions.

1. When does the function achieve a maximum value? What is the maximum value?

2. Suppose someone dives into a pool and you want to model their distance from the surface of the water over time. Which type of curve would you use?

3. What is the answer if you measure distance from the bottom of the pool?

 Calculator Activity 3: Trace

1. Enter the equation $Y_1 = -16x^2 + 60x + 4$ into the calculator and view the resulting graph.

2. The graph models the path of a rocket fired 4 feet above the ground with an initial velocity of 60 feet per second. Trace to several points and describe the rocket at each point. For example, for the point $(1.5, 58)$, at 1.5 seconds the rocket was 58 feet in the air.

Calculator Activity 5: Key Points

1. Enter the equation $Y_1 = -16x^2 + 75x + 4$ into the calculator, modeling the height of a rocket over time. Graph the equation.

2. Find the vertex and the x-intercepts by using the TRACE function.

3. What does the vertex tell you about the rocket?

4. What will the graph look like close to the vertex?

5. What will the table look like close to the vertex?

6. What does the larger x-intercept tell you about the rocket?

7. What will the graph look like close to the x-intercept?

8. What will the table look like close to the x-intercept?

Calculator Activity 6: Finding and Interpreting Velocity

1. a. Enter $Y_1 = -8x(2x - 9)$ into the calculator.

    b. Choose TBLSET. Let TblStart = 1.5 and ΔTbl = 0.25, and then go to the table. Write down two observations.

    c. Predict the value of Y_1 for 1.25 and 3.25. Check to see whether you are right. Does the pattern continue for other values?

    d. Now enter $Y_2 = -(4x - 9)^2 + 81$. What do you notice?

    e. How can you check to see whether the equations are equivalent?

Calculator Activity 7: Using the Correct Equation

Suppose a projectile is fired upward and after 6 seconds reaches its maximum height of 600 feet.

1. a. Write an equation that models the projectile and includes the given conditions. Don't forget the -16 for gravity.

    b. Enter the equation into the calculator. What window values should you use to show the path of the projectile on the screen when you graph?

    c. Use a table to find the initial height of the rocket and the time in the air to the nearest tenth of a second.

2. Repeat the activity for a rocket that reaches its maximum height of 800 feet after 7 seconds. How would you find the initial velocity?

Calculator Activity 8: Initial Velocity

Suppose a fireworks technician fires a rocket upward from an initial height of 5 feet.

1. Graph $Y_1 = 200$ and $Y_2 = -16x^2 + Kx + 5$.

2. Try different values for K. How does the graph of the function change when K changes?

3. What should be the initial velocity in order for the rocket to reach a maximum height of 200 feet?

 Calculator Activity 9: Comparing Tables

1. Generate a table for $y = x^2$ looking at x-values from -3 to 3.

2. Make a sketch of the curve using the points you obtained from the table.

3. Now consider the equation $y = (x - 3)^2$. What x-values do you need to obtain the y-values you got on $y = x^2$?

4. Generate a new table obtaining the y-values with x-values that are 3 bigger.

5. What effect does this have on the original curve?

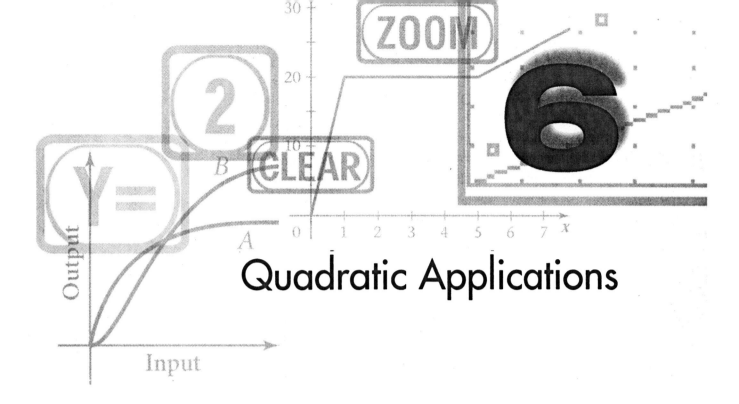

Quadratic Applications

In this chapter, students work with two different applications of quadratic functions. The first application is maximizing the area of a rectangle given a fixed perimeter. The second is distance in feet needed to stop an automobile over speed of the car in miles per hour. As it turns out, these two very different applications have the same form of equation.

The transition all the way from qualitative graphs to equations is quickly accomplished, and the four representations (verbal, numerical, algebraic, and graphical) are interwoven throughout the lessons.

Lesson 1

Area of a Square

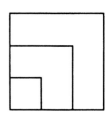

1. Find the graph that best shows the relationship between the **length** of a side of a square and its area. Be careful here. For each unit **increase** in length, is the increase in area the same? Look at the square **to help** you decide. If the increase is the same, then the rate of increase is **a constant** and the graph is linear. If not, the graph is not linear. Write **a few** sentences explaining your choice.

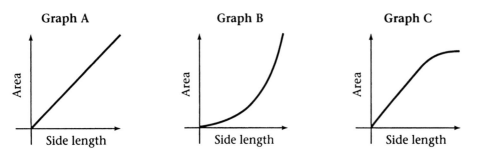

2. The graph below shows the area of a square as a function of the length of one side.

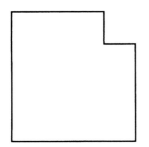

   a. For each of the three points marked on the graph, describe the area and the side length of a square.

   b. Is the y-coordinate always larger than the x-coordinate? Is it true that the square of a number is always bigger than the number? Explain your answer.

3. Jerome has a square piece of paper with an area of 16 square inches. He cuts a corner out of the square as shown.

a. If Jerome cuts larger and larger squares from the same corner, what happens to the area of the original piece of paper?

b. Which graph models the remaining area as a function of the length of the side of the square cut out? Look again at the square to decide whether the rate of decrease is constant.

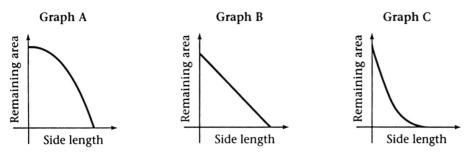

Graph A · Graph B · Graph C

TEACHER NOTES

In this lesson, students begin investigating an application of quadratic functions. Here they explore the length of a side of a square as it relates to its area.

In Question 1, students explore the square of a number. It is a common mistake to think that if you square something, then you automatically get something bigger. Encourage them to compare the graphs of $y = x$ and $y = x^2$.

Question 3 may be difficult for some students because the remaining paper is not square. Explain that they can find the area of the remaining paper by subtracting the area of the cutout from the area of the original square piece of paper. You may want students to model the situation by cutting out larger and larger corners from a square piece of paper and determining the area of the paper left.

Answers

1. Graph B. As the length of the side increases for each unit increase in length, a larger and larger section of area is added. More specifically, when length increases from n to $n + 1$, area increases by $2n + 1$ square units. (Note: $(n + 1)^2 - n^2 = 2n + 1$.)

2. **a.** When the side length is 1.66, the area of the square is 2.76 sq. in. When the side length is 0.4, the area of the square is 0.16 sq. in. When the side length is $\sqrt{3}$, the area of the square is 3 sq. in.

   b. No. In the point (0.4, 0.16), the y-coordinate is smaller than the x-coordinate. If $0 < x < 1$, then $x^2 < x$; if $x > 1$, then $x^2 > x$.

3. **a.** The area decreases.

   b. Graph A

Extension: See Calculator Activity 1

Students use the graphing calculator to investigate a problem similar to Question 3 in the lesson.

A Visual Approach to Functions

TEACHER NOTES (continued)

Answers to Calculator Activity

2. As the area of the square cutout increases, the area remaining decreases.

3.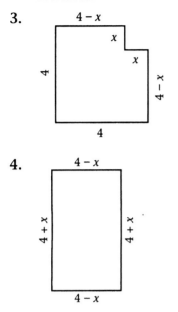

4.

   The area of this figure is found by multiplying the length times the width: $(4 + x)(4 - x) = 16 - x^2$.

5. The equation, $y = 16 - x^2$, is the same as in Question 1.

Lesson 2

Perimeter of a Rectangle

1. Regina made these rectangles with the same piece of string, so the perimeter of each rectangle is the same.

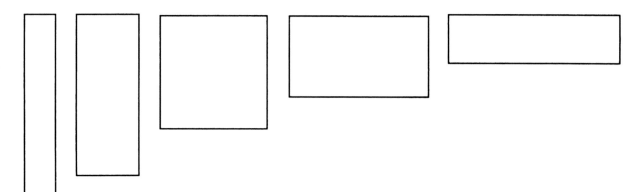

Which sentence describes Regina's rectangles?

    A. As the width of the rectangle increases, the area increases.

    B. As the width of the rectangle increases, the area remains the same.

    C. As the width of the rectangle increases, the area first increases and then decreases.

2. **a.** Using whole number widths, draw as many rectangles as you can with a perimeter of 24. For each rectangle, label the length of each side and give the area.

    b. Make a table of the width, length, and area for all the rectangles you drew.

    c. What do you notice about the sum of length and width? Explain why this is the case.

    d. Choose several points from the table you made in part b. Make a graph showing the relationship of the width and the area. Are there additional points you know will be on the graph? Explain your reasoning.

    e. What happens to the area of the rectangle as the width increases? Explain.

3. Draw a rectangle with a perimeter of 24 where the width is not a whole number. Then find the area of the rectangle. Can one dimension be a whole number and the other not?

A Visual Approach to Functions / © 2002 Key Curriculum Press

TEACHER NOTES

In this lesson, students investigate the relationship of the perimeter of a rectangle to its length and width.

You may need to review whole numbers because students are asked to look at widths that are whole numbers and widths that are not.

Since the perimeter is a constant, to increase the width by 1 unit we must remove 1 unit from the length, as shown.

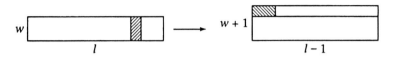

When removing one unit from the length, students can shift a piece of the rectangle from one end to the top and fill in the area to make the shape a rectangle whenever $w < l - 1$. This means the area will increase whenever $w < l - 1$. The larger the difference is between w and $l - 1$, the greater the amount of area there is to fill in to make the shape a rectangle. Similarly, if $w > l - 1$, then the area of the new rectangle will be smaller as they will have to cut off a portion of the shifted rectangle. We will return to the notion of increasing and decreasing area in the next lesson.

Answers

1. Sentence C

2. a.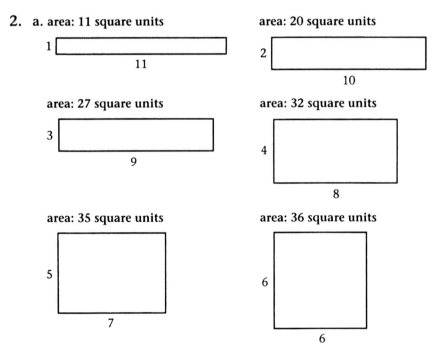

b.

Width	Length	Area
1	11	11
2	10	20
3	9	27
4	8	32
5	7	35
6	6	36

c. The sum of the length and width is always 12. We know that
$2w + 2l = 24$, so $w + l = 12$.

d.

(6, 36)
(5, 35) (7, 35)
(4, 32) (8, 32)
(3, 27) (9, 27)
(2, 20) (10, 20)
(1, 11) (11, 11)

Length and width can be reversed, so additional points are (7, 35),
(8, 32), (9, 27), (10, 20), (11, 11).

e. With the perimeter of the rectangles remaining the same, as the width
increases, the area increases until the width becomes larger than the
length. At this point, the area begins to decrease.

3. Answers will vary. It is not possible for one dimension to be a whole
number and the other not as $l + w = 12$, so $l = 12 - w$.

🔲 *Extension: See Calculator Activity 2* _____

Answers to Calculator Activity

3. The line gives the length for a chosen width.

4. The parabola gives the area.

Lesson 3
Fixed Perimeter

Grandma's Fencing Company sells a type of fencing made up of 32 sections connected with hinges. The fencing is flexible, so it can enclose different-sized areas.

1. Suppose the sections are placed to form a rectangle. What is the perimeter of the rectangle in sections?

2. Make a table of the dimensions of all the rectangles you can form. In your table, list the length, width, and area of each rectangle. What do you notice about the perimeter of each rectangle?

3. Make a graph showing width versus area using the dimensions from Question 2.

4. Imagine a horizontal line, $y = c$, drawn on the graph from Question 3.

   a. If the line $y = c$ intersects the curve twice and one point of intersection is (a, c), what is the other point of intersection? What does this tell you?

   b. What does it mean when the line intersects the curve only once?

   c. What does it mean when the line doesn't intersect the curve?

5. Darrin and Lou each enclosed a section in their yards using the flexible fencing described at the beginning of the lesson.

   a. If both sections have the same area, do you think their dimensions (length and width) are the same? Explain.

   b. Darrin wants to enclose the largest section of his yard possible. What will be the dimensions of the enclosed section? Justify your claim.

6. Which of these equations gives the correct area for a rectangle with a perimeter of 32? Let $A(x)$ stand for area and x stand for width.

   A. $A(x) = x(32 - x)$

   B. $A(x) = x(16 - x)$

   C. $A(x) = x(32 - 2x)$

Suppose you have a rectangle with a fixed perimeter. These pictures show what happens when you remove 1 unit from the length and add it to the width for a rectangle where $w < l - 1$.

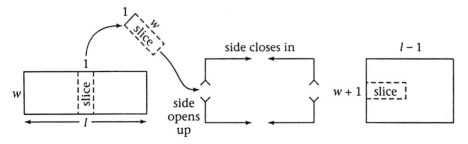

Consider the three different cases in Questions 7–9. For each case, do you need to add, subtract, or maintain the same area to get the slice to complete the rectangle?

7. $w < l - 1$

8. $w = l - 1$

9. $w > l - 1$

Suppose that the width of a rectangle is less than its length by an amount d. That is, $l = w + d$. A slice with sides w and $\frac{1}{2}d$ has been removed from the rectangle on the left and moved to the top of the remaining (closed-up) rectangle to help form the rectangle on the right.

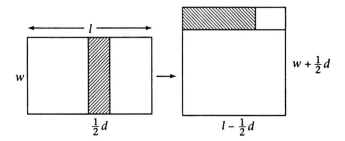

10. Write a few sentences explaining why the new rectangle to the right of the arrow has the same perimeter but larger area than the rectangle to the left of the arrow.

11. Give the dimensions of each of the three pieces that make up the rectangle on the right. What special type of figure is the new rectangle? Why?

12. If you now try to increase the width while you keep the perimeter constant, what will happen to the area?

 A Visual Approach to Functions / © 2002 Key Curriculum Press

TEACHER NOTES

The focus of this lesson is to investigate an area with a constant perimeter.

Students may benefit from a discussion of how to derive the equation for area given that a rectangle has a fixed perimeter p. You can use the question below to help facilitate the discussion.

1. Suppose a and b are the dimensions of a rectangle with a perimeter of 24 units.

   a. Write an equation you know to be true about the rectangle.

   b. Use the equation to write b in terms of a.

   c. Now express the area of the rectangle in terms of a.

2. Suppose c and d are the dimensions of a second rectangle with a perimeter of 24 units.

   a. Express the area of this rectangle in terms of c.

   b. If the areas of this rectangle and the rectangle in Question 1 are equal, you can set the two expressions for area equal to each other.

   c. What does this tell you about rectangles that have the same perimeter and area?

Answers

1. 32 sections

2.

Length	Width	Area
1	15	15
2	14	28
3	13	39
4	12	48
5	11	55
6	10	60
7	9	63
8	8	64

The perimeter is 32 for each of the rectangles.

3.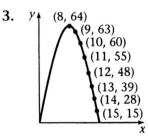

4. **a.** If $0 < c < 64$, there are two points of intersection, one point (a, c) and the other $(16 - a, c)$ signifying that two congruent rectangles with a perimeter of 32 have an area equal to c. (One has width a and length $16 - a$ while the other has width $16 - a$ and length a.)

   b. If $c = 64$, there is one point of intersection meaning that exactly one rectangle with a perimeter of 32 has an area of 64. This is the 8×8 square.

   c. When $c > 64$, there will be no intersection meaning that no rectangle with a perimeter of 32 has an area bigger than 64 square units.

5. **a.** Yes. The rectangles are congruent.

   b. 8×8. The largest area occurs when $w = l = \left(\frac{1}{4}\right)p$.

6. Equation B

7. Add area

8. Maintain the same area

9. Subtract area

10. For both rectangles the perimeter is $2l + 2w$, but the upper right corner piece was added to the area.

11. $w \times \left(l - \frac{1}{2}d\right)$, $w \times \frac{1}{2}d$, and $\frac{1}{2}d \times \frac{1}{2}d$; a square, because $l = w + d$ implies that $l - \frac{1}{2}d = w + \frac{1}{2}d$

12. The area will decrease. For an increase in width, we would have to slice off a section of length in order to maintain a constant perimeter. When we move this section to the top, we would have to cut off a piece of the area.

Lesson 4

Maximizing Area

1. Suppose a rectangle has a perimeter of 20 centimeters. What is the area if the width is 0.5 centimeter? What is the area if the width is 3 centimeters? What dimensions lead to maximum area?

2. Suppose another rectangle has a perimeter of 25 centimeters. Can both dimensions be whole numbers? Explain why or why not. What dimensions lead to the maximum area for this rectangle?

3. Suppose an $a \times b$ rectangle has a perimeter p where p is a whole number. For what choices of p are a and b not whole numbers? Hint: You may want to make a chart starting with $p = 1$ and find all the possible values for a and b where both a and b are whole numbers. Keep increasing p until you see a pattern.

TEACHER NOTES

In this lesson, students continue investigating rectangles with a fixed perimeter. They also explore when the length and width of rectangles can or cannot be integers.

Answers

1. The area is 4.75 square centimeters when the width is 0.5 centimeter. The area is 21 square centimeters when the width is 3 centimeters. The 5×5 square leads to the greatest area.

2. It is not possible for both dimensions to be whole numbers. We know the sum of length and width is 12.5 centimeters, so it is impossible for both length and width to be integers. The 6.25×6.25 square has the greatest area.

3. For p equal to any odd integer, there are no dimensions where both a and b are whole numbers. We know the sum of length and width is $p/2$, which is not an integer if p is odd. If $p = 2$, again there are no whole-number dimensions because length plus width is 1. Otherwise, dimensions can have whole-number lengths.

⌨ Extension: See Calculator Activity 4 _____

Students have looked at many examples where perimeter is fixed and area varies. Here they look at the situation where area is fixed and perimeter varies.

Answers to Calculator Activity

1–2.

Width	Length	Perimeter
1	36	74
2	18	40
3	12	30
4	9	26
6	6	24

5. $y = 2x + 2\left(\frac{36}{x}\right)$ where y is the perimeter and x is a dimension.

3. The numbers descend. It looks like the square has the smallest perimeter.

4. If you increase the width of a square when the perimeter is fixed, you lose area. In order to maintain area and increase the width, you would have to add perimeter.

6.

Lesson 5

More on Maximizing Area

Suppose 1000 feet of fence is available to create three sides of a rectangular enclosure for animals along a river. No fencing is needed along the river, which serves as the fourth side.

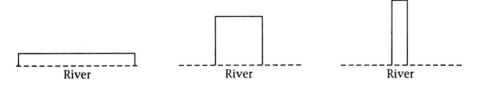

1. Which sentence describes the relationship between the width of the enclosure, measured perpendicular to the river, and the area?

   A. As the width of the enclosure increases the area increases.

   B. As the width of the enclosure increases the area remains the same.

   C. As the width of the enclosure increases the area first increases and then decreases.

2. Which graph matches the correct description in Question 1?

   Graph A   **Graph B**   **Graph C**

   (Graph A: Area vs. Width — increasing line; Graph B: Area vs. Width — horizontal line; Graph C: Area vs. Width — parabola peaking)

   We want to discover which dimensions will lead to maximum enclosed area. As before, we will increase the width w by taking from the length l (the side parallel to the river). To increase the width by d units we remove two pieces as shown below.

3.

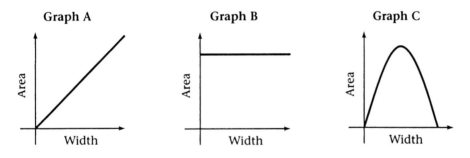

   What is the new width? The new length?

4. When does the process above lead to a smaller area for the enclosure? To a larger area? Does the process ever lead to the same area?

5. Why is it necessary to remove two pieces instead of only one? Explain the difference between this problem and a situation that requires fencing on all four sides. What dimensions give the maximum area?

6. Consider the case in which two identical adjacent pens are enclosed as in the figure below. Given a fixed perimeter, which dimensions lead to maximum area?

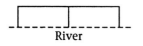
River

7. Can you generalize your results in Question 6 to three or more identical adjacent pens with fixed perimeter?

Lesson 5 is an advanced topic typically treated in calculus classes. With a visual approach, students see how the solutions make sense in physical terms. They can get the dimensions needed to optimize an enclosure without using calculus.

Answers

1–2. As with the case in which the entire rectangle is enclosed, Sentence C is the correct description and Graph C the correct shape.

3. The new width is $w + d$. The new length is $l - 2d$.

4. The process will lead to a smaller area if $2w > l - 2d$. It will lead to a larger area if $2w < l - 2d$. It will lead to the same area if $2w = l - 2d$.

5. Two slices must be removed because we are drawing from a single length to build up two widths. The maximum area occurs if $2w = l$, because for $2w < l$ we can always create a new rectangle with more area by cutting down on l, but with $2w = l$ this is no longer possible.

6. When building up the widths three slices must be removed from the top since we are drawing from one single length to build up three widths. By the argument given in Question 4, the maximum area occurs if $3w = l$, because for $3w < l$ we can always create a new rectangle with more area by cutting down on l, but with $3w = l$ this is no longer possible.

7. With k adjacent pens we will have $k + 1$ widths and, as above for fixed perimeter, the maximum area will occur when $(k + 1)w = l$. Now $(k + 1)w + l = P$, so $w = 0.5P/(k + 1)$ and $l = 0.5P$.

Extension: See Calculator Activity 5 _____

If students enjoy this exercise you can choose a different fixed area and go through the development again.

TEACHER NOTES

Answers to Calculator Activity

1.

Width	Length	Perimeter
1	72	146
2	36	76
3	24	54
4	18	44
6	12	36
8	9	34

2. There is no square whose sides have integer length that has a fixed area of 72, because 72 is not a perfect square number.

3. $y = 2x + 2\left(\frac{72}{x}\right)$

Lesson 6

Braking Distance and Speed

The distance a car travels after the driver applies the brakes until it stops is called the "braking distance." Look at the chart showing the braking distance of a car at three different speeds.

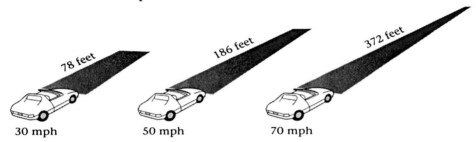

Notice that the distance does not increase by equal amounts even though the speed does. In fact, the braking distance increases in the same way the area of a square does when the length of the sides is increased.

1. The graphs show the braking distance as a function of the speed of two cars. Choose the graph that best matches each sentence. Write a sentence explaining your reasoning.

   a. The braking distance of a car increases as the speed increases, and the rate of change of the braking distance also increases as the speed increases.

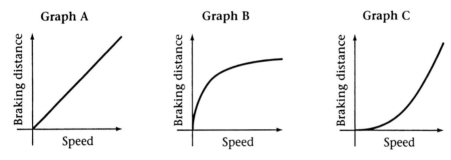

   b. Lupe discovered that when she drives 60 miles per hour (mph), it takes 162 feet to stop. She also found that when she drives 40 mph, it takes 72 feet to stop.

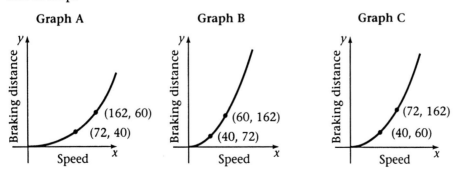

2. Which table best matches the sentence in Question 1a? Explain.

Speed (mph)	Braking Distance (feet)
0	0
10	4.5
20	18
30	40.5
40	72

Table A

Speed (mph)	Braking Distance (feet)
0	0
10	27
20	48
30	63
40	72

Table B

Speed (mph)	Braking Distance (feet)
0	0
10	18
20	36
30	54
40	72

Table C

3. Choose the table from Question 2 that matches each equation. Let x be the speed and y be the braking distance.

a. $y = 1.8x$

b. $y = 0.045x^2$

c. $y = -0.03x^2 + 3x$

TEACHER NOTES

This lesson introduces students to another application of quadratic functions. The focus is on relating the tables and graphs of quadratic functions to equations, using real-world applications.

Students may have difficulty interpreting the graphs to determine how the rate of change is increasing.

Point out to students that they are looking at braking distance as a function of speed. So, for each point on the curve, the *x*-coordinate represents speed and the *y*-coordinate represents braking distance.

In math, we say that the braking distance increases as the square of speed.

Answers

1. **a.** Graph C. Only Graph C is increasing with an increasing rate of change.

   b. Graph B. The graph includes the points (40, 72) and (60, 162).

2. Table A is the only table with an increasing rate of change. (Table B has a decreasing rate of change, and Table C has a constant rate of change.)

3. **a.** Table C   **b.** Table A   **c.** Table B

Extension: See Calculator Activity 6

Students need practice figuring out whether a function is increasing or decreasing and whether its rate of change is increasing or decreasing by looking at various graphs and tables of values. It is helpful to draw the graphs on the board. Increasing and concave up denotes increasing with an increasing rate of change. Increasing and concave down denotes increasing with a decreasing rate of change. Decreasing and concave up denotes decreasing with an increasing rate of change. Decreasing and concave down denotes decreasing with a decreasing rate of change.

Students should use graphing calculators when they work on the questions so that they learn to detect increasing and decreasing rates of change from the table for a function.

Answers to Calculator Activity

2. Y1 and Y4 are increasing, because when *x*-values increase so do *y*-values. Y2 and Y3 are decreasing because when *x*-values increase *y*-values decrease.

3. The rates of change of Y1 and Y3 are increasing because as *x*-values increase, the change in *y*-values increases. The rates of change of Y2 and Y4 are decreasing because as *x*-values increase, the change in *y*-values decreases.

Lesson 7

The Braking Distance Equation

The braking distance on dry pavement for a driver with normal reactions is modeled by the equation $D = 0.045v^2$ where v is the speed in miles per hour and D is the braking distance in feet.

The graph shows the braking distance of a car as a function of speed.

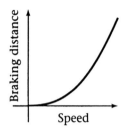

1. **a.** Fiona is driving at a speed of 25 mph. What is the braking distance?

   b. What point on the curve does this correspond to?

2. **a.** After Jack applies his brakes, his car travels 200 feet before it comes to a complete stop. How fast was the car traveling?

   b. What point on the curve does this correspond to?

3. Explain how to solve Question 2a graphically and algebraically.

A Visual Approach to Functions / © 2002 Key Curriculum Press

TEACHER NOTES

In this lesson, students continue to look at the relationship between braking distance and speed.

Question 3 asks students to find the speed of a car, given the braking distance, both algebraically and graphically. Finding the answer algebraically should not be difficult. Students may need assistance in finding the answer graphically.

Answers

1. a. The braking distance for a car going 25 mph is 28.125 ft.

   b. The exact point on the curve is (25, 28.125).

2. a. If a car takes 200 ft to stop, it was going about 67 mph.

   b. The point on the curve is (66.67, 200).

3. To solve the problem graphically, let $Y_1 = 0.045x^2$ and $Y_2 = 200$, and look where the two curves intersect. Also, you could trace along the Y_1 curve until the y-coordinate is 200. To solve the problem algebraically, solve the equation $200 = 0.045x^2$.

Extension: See Calculator Activity 7 _____

Students repeat the questions in the lesson, this time using more difficult values.

Answers to Calculator Activity

1. 49.5 feet   2. 58.5 feet   3. 67.5 feet

Lesson 8

Doubling Your Speed

The braking distance on dry pavement for a driver with normal reactions is modeled by the equation $D = 0.045v^2$ where v is the speed in miles per hour and D is the braking distance in feet.

1. Imagine you are driving to school. Select your speed. Then approximate the distance it would take you to stop your car. Justify your answer.

2. What happens to your braking distance when you double your speed?

3. Imagine that you triple your speed in Question 1. What is the ratio of the braking distance in Question 1 to the braking distance at triple the original speed? Explain.

4. Two cars are headed toward each other. One car is traveling at 35 mph and the other at 55 mph. How far apart must the two cars be when the drivers step on the brakes in order to avoid a collision? Explain your answer.

TEACHER NOTES

In this lesson, students continue to explore the braking distance of a car with respect to the speed.

For Questions 2 and 3, it may help students to create a table of values in order to see the effect of doubling and tripling the speed.

For Question 4, students must find how far apart two cars traveling toward each other must be when the drivers apply the brakes in order to avoid a collision. (Students may mistakenly subtract rather than add.) Encourage them to draw a picture as part of the explanation.

Answers

1. Answers will vary depending on the speed used. If the speed driven is 30 mph, the braking distance is 40.5 feet.

2. Doubling the speed quadruples the braking distance.

3. If you triple the speed, the ratio of the two braking distances is 1 to 9. Assume one driver is going at v mph; then the braking distance is $0.045v^2$. Now if someone goes 3 times as fast, the speed is $3v$. This person's braking distance then is $0.045(3v)^2 = 0.045(9v^2)$, which is 9 times the original braking distance.

4. The cars must be at least 192 feet apart because $0.045(55)^2 + 0.045(35)^2 = 191.25$.

Extension: See Calculator Activity 8 _____

Answers to Calculator Activity

1. The braking distances are 16, 25, and 36 times as far.
2. The braking distance is k^2 as far.

▣ Calculator Activity 1: Area Equations

1. On a graphing calculator, graph $y = 16 - x^2$. Use an x-min of 0 and an x-max of 4.7. Let y range from 0 to 20. The graph represents the area remaining when a square of side length x is cut out of a square of side length 4 units.

2. Choose three points along the curve. Describe the square with the cutout using the coordinates of the points. (Example: When a square of length 2.5 inches is cut out of the corner of a square that is 16 square inches, the remaining area is 9.75 square inches.)

3. Now draw the figure. Label the sides using x for the dimension of the cutout.

4. Now imagine slicing off one side of the cutout and rearranging the pieces to form a rectangle. Draw the resulting rectangle. Label the sides and find the area using the dimensions of the rectangle.

5. How does the equation for the area of the rectangle compare to the original equation from Question 1?

▣ Calculator Activity 2: Interpreting Perimeter and Area Graphs

1. Graph the line $y = 12 - x$ and the parabola $y = x(12 - x)$. Use the settings x-min = 0 and x-max = 18.8 to produce clean trace values.

2. Carefully examine each graph.

3. What does the line tell you about the rectangle?

4. What does the parabola tell you about the rectangle?

5. Now, pressing TRACE and jumping from one curve to the other, make statements about the rectangle. For example: If the width of a rectangle with a fixed perimeter of 24 is 9.4, then the length is 2.6 and the area is 24.44.

Calculator Activity 4: Fixed Area

We have looked at many examples where perimeter is fixed and area varies. Let's look at the situation where area is fixed and perimeter varies.

1. Suppose the area is 36. Make a table with the dimensions for a rectangle with a fixed area of 36. Don't include repeating perimeters.

2. For each width in the table, give the perimeter of the rectangle.

3. What observations can you make about the list?

4. Does your observation make sense? Explain.

5. Can you come up with an equation that gives the perimeter for all rectangles with a fixed area of 36?

6. Graph this equation on a graphing calculator using a window suggested by your table above. You can let *x* vary from 0 to 18.8 to get nice trace values.

 Calculator Activity 5: Varying Perimeter

We have looked at many examples where perimeter is fixed and area varies. What if we want to look at a situation where area is fixed and perimeter varies?

1. Suppose the area is 72. Make a table using whole-number dimensions for a rectangle with a fixed area of 72. You know the only possible widths are all the divisors of 72: 1, 2, 3, 4, 6, 8, 9, 12, 18, 24, 36, and 72. For each width on the list give the perimeter of the rectangle.

2. What observations can you make about the list? Why does this make sense?

3. Can you come up with an equation that gives the perimeter for all rectangles of fixed area 72? Graph it on a graphing calculator using a window suggested by your list above. If you let *x* vary from 0 to 18.8, you get nice trace values. Use the graph to come up with various perimeters for the rectangle.

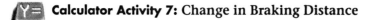

Calculator Activity 6: Increasing or Decreasing

1. Graph the following equations: $Y_1 = 3(1.2^x)$, $Y_2 = 5(0.8^x)$, $Y_3 = -Y_1$, $Y_4 = -Y_2$. Let x range from 0 to 10 and let y range from -10 to 10.

2. For each function, decide whether the function is increasing or decreasing. Explain how you know.

3. For each function, decide whether the rate of change is increasing or decreasing. Explain how you know.

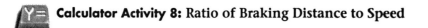

Calculator Activity 7: Change in Braking Distance

Refer to Lesson 7 to find the difference in braking distance when you increase speed

1. from 50 to 60 mph.

2. from 60 to 70 mph.

3. from 70 to 80 mph.

Calculator Activity 8: Ratio of Braking Distance to Speed

In the lesson, you found the ratio of the braking distance to speed when you double and triple your speed. Enter $Y_1 = 0.045x^2$ and look at your table values.

1. By what factor does your braking distance increase if you are going 4, 5, or 6 times as fast?

2. By what factor does your braking distance increase if you are going k times as fast?